The Story Matters

Compiled by
Tammie Price
President & Founder

A Place for Us Ministries, Inc. P.O. Box 797
Greenwood, S.C. 29648

PRESS

The Story Matters
true stories of radical faith, courage, struggles, and survival
by Tammie Price

Printed in the United States of America

ISBN 9781622303021

Unless otherwise indicated, Bible quotations are taken from The American King James Version; The New International Version. Copyright © 1973, 1978,1984, 2011 by Biblica, Inc.; The God's Word. Copyright © 1995 by Baker Publishing Group; The Message. Copyright © 1993, 1994, 1995. 1996, 2000, 2001, 2002 by NavPress Publishing Group; The New Living Translation. Copyright © 1996, 2004, 2007 by Tyndale House Foundation; The New King James Version. Copyright © 1982 by Thomas Nelson, Inc.; The English Standard Version. Copyright © 2001, 2007 by Crossway Bibles (of Good News Publishers); and The Amplified Bible. Copyright © 1954, 1958, 1962, 1964, 1965, 1987 by The Lockman Foundation.

A Place for Us
Words and Music by Jimmy Scott and Wayne Tester
Copyright © 1997 Universal Music Corp., NO WAYNE NO GAIN
    MUSIC, CHRYSALIS MUSIC and STONE ANGEL MUSIC
All Rights for NO WAYNE NO GAIN MUSIC Controlled and
    Administered by UNIVERSAL MUSIC CORP.
All Rights for CHRYSALIS MUSIC and STONE ANGEL MUSIC
    Administered by BMG RIGHTS MANAGEMENT (US) LLC

Dedication

To the Residents:

This book is dedicated to every brave resident who left her surroundings, family, and friends (and whatever else made her feel secure) to enter the program at A Place for Us Ministries. Despite your questions, tears, doubts, and fears, you made the difficult decision to give up many privileges. You knew in your heart that it was time to make some brave life changes. For you, it may have been a sacrifice and selfless act of love for your unborn baby, or it might have been a matter of life or death for yourself. We hope that the things you learned will forever change your life. Thanks to each one of you who changed our lives forever. You are our heroes.

To the Babies:

To the babies that were given life while your mother lived in our home, your mother and the staff at A Place for Us Ministries cherish the day you took your first breath. You were precious in your mother's sight. You could see it in her eyes, sense it in her touch, and hear it through her words. Through much prayer, your mother made the decision to make a parenting plan. She worked hard to provide a stable environment for you so that you could have a place to call home. For others, once your mother knew that the Lord had another plan for you, her emotions burst with wailing cries from her heart of despair. Always know that your mother loved you more than life itself. It was with much grief that she released you into the arms of a loving family. Her heart went with you that day. I will never forget the mother who sang to her beautiful daughter as she was preparing to release her to the adoptive family. As tears streamed down her face she sang, "Alina, Mommy's little girl in a big, big world. You deserve the best, big diamonds and pearls." She hugged her little girl and said, "Alina, I love you!" What a selfless act of love! Our prayer is that one day we will see each of you fulfilling the purpose God had for your life even before conception.

Acknowledgements

God has placed some very special people with different talents together so that stories that matter could be compiled into a book. We are truly grateful for all those who agreed to share their stories. <u>Their names are not listed here because many names were changed in order to protect their privacy</u>. We are also thankful for each person who gave time, labor, or resources throughout the planning and building of this ministry and the role you played in these (and many more) God Stories. One kind donor and volunteer said, "God just needs His people to do His work." We thank all the people who came together to do this work, becoming the hands and feet to the vision that God gave for this ministry. There were so many churches, civic organizations, volunteers, and financial or prayer partners who have made amazing contributions to this ministry who are not mentioned in this book. You know who you are, and so does God. We are forever grateful to each helpful hand and praying heart that has partnered with us in this endeavor!

First, I would like to thank **our Lord and Savior, Jesus Christ,** Who gave us the time, talents, and the resources to write and publish this book. It has been a dream from the beginning of A Place for Us Ministries. Once we began to see all the God stories, we knew that one day we would have the opportunity to share them through a book. To God be the glory for the things He has done!

To the Board of Directors: Thank you for walking in faith and obedience to the leading of the Holy Spirit to answer this call—not always knowing what would come next but always waiting upon the Lord to direct our next step. Although we have seen many things come to pass over the last ten years, we know that God is not finished yet. There are many other dreams and visions that have not been fulfilled, and we wait expectantly to see what the next step will be. We have believed in God to meet our every need; He is Jehovah Jireh, our Provider. There were seasons we heard, "Be still and know that I am God." In doing so, we embarked on a journey we will never forget, and along the way, we have learned that "with God, all things are possible!"(Matthew 19:26 NIV) Thank you for being supportive of the writing of this book and for voting to say, "Let's do it!"

To the Families of all who worked on this book: Thank you for being patient and understanding as we took time away from you and our other responsibilities. **A special thank you to my family for allowing me to share "my story" which included all of you. By the way, each one of you is a part of why my story matters. Thank you for being you!**

To Kimberly Overcast: Thank you for all the endless hours of writing, editing and the gathering of many stories. Words can never express our gratitude to you for helping us get this book started!

To Pat and Susan Jordan: Just when we thought we had the book ready for the publishers, Susan, you came to the beauty shop for one of those divine appointments. After talking with Pat, we found there was much work to be done. What a blessing the two of you have been! Pat, you taught us how to make the stories come to life. We added details to describe the personalities of those in the stories and tried to incorporate the five senses because of your expertise. Thanks for sharing your opinion with us.

To Andrea Southerland: Thank you for your diligence in editing the stories while being so patient, sending them out to be proofed and then allowing me to change something "just one more time." You have done an outstanding job!

To Suzanne Carroll: Your writing gift was a blessing just when we needed it. Thanks for your sacrifice of time even during a difficult time in your life. May your giving come back "pressed down, shaken together and running over" (Luke 6:38 NIV).

To Lesa Jefferies: Thank you for all the long hours both day and night that you gave to make sure this book would touch as many lives as possible. You are one of the greatest examples of selfless giving that I know. Thank you for using your gift of writing, design work, and "Photography by Lesa" to bless this ministry and the publishing of this book.

To Amy Boyer: Thank you for compiling the resource and citing page. We know that many lives will be changed through these valuable resources. We are honored to have you on our team.

To all those who took time to proof this book: May God bless your lives richly. **Allison Moore, Lillian Moneyhun, Sandi Southerland, Lauren Ulrich, and Joyce Alexander,** thank you for your diligence and time to join us in this book-writing endeavor. We could not have done it without you!

To our Prayer Partners: We are forever thankful that you joined your faith with ours. Prayer has been the backbone of this ministry and has gotten many residents, staff, and board members through challenging decisions. We have a prayer team of over four hundred people, many of which have covered this ministry in prayer since inception. Thank you for your prayers over this book.

To the Staff: I am greatly indebted to the staff of A Place for Us and The Alcoves. Many came on board not seeking a "job" but a "calling." Staff members have worked endless hours, sometimes with little or no pay, to do the job before them. I extend my gratitude to you for the care that you have given to each resident of A Place for Us and each customer of The Alcoves. By doing this you have extended the love and hope of Christ Jesus. You too are a reason we are able to tell the story.

To the Moneyhun Family: The use of your beach house was an answer to prayer. We enjoyed the walks on the beach, the fellowship and the presence of the Lord that filled your home as we worked to write over half of this book. We are forever grateful to your family for all the ways you have blessed this ministry and touched our lives.

To Kim Hill: We are honored by the foreword you wrote about APFUM and *The Story Matters*. Thank you for taking time out of your busy schedule to partner with this ministry. You have used your gift of singing, speaking, and writing to bless our lives along with many others. We are thankful God connected us with you over ten years ago when we heard you singing A Place for Us. We are forever grateful for your kindness and generosity.

To the Endorsers: We are truly thankful for the beautifully written endorsements, thank you for taking time out to partner with us in this endeavor. Thanks again, **Angela Thomas, John Potter, Jeff Duncan, Sheila Cornea, Rod Schultz, Archie Moore,** and **Nick Cunningham**.

To the People: I am thankful for all the people over the past ten years that said, "You have got to write a book!" Your words of encouragement erased all the fear and intimidation of such a great task and enabled us to write down each account, knowing that the story mattered. Because of many of you, I got out my journals where I recorded answered prayers, testimonies, and the history of this ministry. Many worked on this book, but without those journals, we could have never been able to recall all the "God" stories that happened over the last ten years. Looking over them, I realized that even the stories that fill the pages of this book do not come close to telling the full extent of His greatness and all He has done over the years.

To the Anonymous Giver: Thank you for your giving and the obedience to listen and know when it is needed. During the writing of this book, we could easily have written another chapter. God continued to show us that he was the author, and he would supply for the printing. Once the book was near completion, we thought about having a fashion show to raise money to help print the books. We still needed about $2,000.00. After talking it over, we felt a fashion show would be too much work for too little money. We decided to believe that God would provide through another avenue. This was on a Wednesday. That Friday, you sent a check for $2,000.00. Thank you for helping us to print books that will lead others to a greater faith.

Table of Contents

Foreword

by Kim Hill

For the past 24 years, I've been in ministry singing around the world. For the better part of the past 15 years, my circle has been the Christian women's conference world. I've loved being part of very large events sponsored by Focus on the Family in arenas with 20,000 women as much as being part of a small-town church's very first attempt at a women's conference where they packed out the church with 200 women.

But there is one thing I've learned in these years that always breaks my heart, and I believe breaks God's heart. From Seattle to South Africa, unfortunately, the common denominator in the room at every conference is pain. The disappointment and despair—that somewhere along the line, life has not turned out as planned or expected. One of my favorite parts of the day is when women share their stories with me, and I have a chance to listen, to cry, and then to pray with them.

But the hard part is that I've heard more stories than I can count about childhood abuse or teenage pregnancy or abortion and the effects it has on women who endure it, even 40 or 50 years later. Every time I hear a heartbreaking story from an older woman, I think, "Why couldn't someone have helped her when she was young to avoid these years of compounding wounds and abuses?"

Beth Moore, who's arguably one of the most effective and beloved Bible teachers in the past decade, is one of the many women I've heard speak about the damage that abuse can bring upon a life. Beth says, "Many wonderful things happened to me as a child. I was loved. I was raised in the church. But I'm not convinced there's enough good to offset the devastation of abuse." Beth, along with countless other well-known women in ministry and the "not so well-known" women that I've had the privilege to meet with at conferences, will say that it took a long time to break free from self-destruction and despair in order to truly live healthy lives.

I was so inspired by several women's stories I heard on the road that I wrote and recorded a song about the shame and wasted years that so many women (inside and outside of the church) live in for decades. I guess that's why when I first heard of A Place for Us and the ministry they were doing with young women, I was thrilled to do anything they wanted me to do. I've had the opportunity to personally meet many of the girls whose stories are written in this precious book. Their faces and songs are etched in my heart. I've also spent time with the women behind the scenes who are literally pouring their lives into this ministry and these young women's lives. I've been humbled by their extravagant love towards girls that so many times the church doesn't embrace at a time when it is so desperately needed.

My connection with A Place for Us Ministries began years ago when the ministry used a song I recorded as their theme song for the ministry. As a result, I've been a musical guest at one of their fundraising banquets and on the platform at their first conference for women in the community of Greenwood, South Carolina. I had the joy of hearing the story of one girl's salvation when a few of them came to a conference that I was part of at The Cove. I've also had the opportunity to visit their beautiful home and have felt the love while sitting around their dinner table enjoying some of Ms. Mamie's home cooking! It has truly been one of my favorite experiences in my life to be a tiny part of their story.

I wish every town in every part of the world had a safe place for young girls like A Place for Us. I know their stories will inspire you the way they've inspired me. I hope you'll join them in their efforts and that you will listen to the Lord for ways that you can step out and do something to help the thousands of girls like the ones in this book whose stories matter!

Blessings,
Kim

Kim Hill is a Grammy-nominated, multi-Dove Award-winning artist with seventeen CD's to her credit. Kim is also the author of <u>Hope No Matter What</u>*, an interactive devotional designed for single parents and their young children to do together after experiencing the trauma of divorce. Kim lives in Franklin, Tennessee, with her two teenage sons.*

Endorsements

S everal years ago, I had the privilege of meeting residents and hearing some of the God stories about A Place for Us Ministries. I believe you will truly be inspired as you read *The Story Matters.*

Angela Thomas, Best-selling Author and Speaker

In the book of Acts, Chapter 17 verse 26, The New International Version says, "From one man, he made every nation of men that they should inhabit the whole earth; and he determined the times set for them and the exact places where they should live."

What's amazing about this verse is that it indicates from the time of the creation of Adam, and then on to every person to inhabit the Earth since him, that God Himself has been intricately involved with His creation —so much so, that He personally assumed the responsibility of being our true lifetime real estate agent!

In this book, *The Story Matters*, we get a glimpse of seeing just how much God does care about where His children dwell! As you read these pages from the unique vantage point of the players in the story of A Place for Us Ministries, you will feel the very presence of God warm your heart like a cozy blanket on a bitterly cold day. This book chronicles the miracles of God bringing something out of nothing in His quest to provide mothers and mothers-to-be with a safe haven and a wellspring of Life!

This story will magnify again just how big our God is and how much He loves taking the needle of hope and the thread of faith and weaving a dream into reality for reaching the last, the least, and the lost. You will cry and laugh (often at the same time) as you experience the reality of the Father's unlimited and often unexpected provision as He architects the dream of this home and ministry. Yes, the story does matter, for the narrator is none other than God Himself and the cast are His children, the apples of His eye! I say, "Well done!"

Jonathan S. Potter
Author, *Spiritual Identity Fraud–Restoring God's Sons and Daughters*

The first time I had the chance to visit A Place for Us Ministries, I immediately felt the love, sense of family, and safety that comes from belonging to a caring home. A Place for Us is a ministry where the Truth is taught, and Christ's love is lived out through Tammie, the staff, and all the volunteers. At this ministry, we see lives being rescued and given a second chance and can witness God's blessings every day. We need more programs like A Place for Us, and we need more people like you to support ministries like this one with your time, your talents, your prayers, and your gifts.

God Bless,
Congressman Jeff Duncan SC-3

"'For I know the plans I have for you,' declares the Lord, 'plans to prosper you and not to harm you, plans to give you hope and a future'" (Jeremiah 29:11 NIV).

A Place for Us Ministries has beautifully depicted the unfolding of many miracles in this heartfelt book, which chronicles the dream of a ministry home becoming a reality. The stories shared by the young women served by this ministry will inspire both those who dare to make positive changes in their lives as well as those who desire to be change agents in the world. Your faith will be stirred, and your heart will be touched by this inspiring book.

Dr. Sheila Cornea
Inspirational Communicator & Coach
Gutsy Grace Resources

I am excited to finally see Tammie's story on paper. *The Story Matters* will bless you as the writer gives us an honest glimpse of her journey through the trials and triumphs of life. This is not just a book but a tool for mending lives.

Rod Schultz, Pastor
Grace Community Church

My heart "shouts with gladness and overflows with thankfulness" to Christ for birthing and growing the powerful, life-changing ministry of A Place for Us. I strongly and highly recommend individuals, groups, and church-fellowships to support their tremendous ministry through prayer, encouragement and "generous, hilarious giving."

Archie Moore, Pastor
Greenwood Presbyterian Church (PCA)

The dedicated servants at A Place for us Ministries serve as a constant reminder of where following Jesus should lead us. God does not call us to the comfortable or to the convenient but instead invites us to follow Him into the broken places and partner with Him in putting the pieces back together. *The Story Matters* serves as a powerful testimony to the relentless life-changing power of God's love and grace.

Nick Cunningham, Teaching Pastor
Ginghamsburg Church

The Shoes Matter

Introduction

I'm an open book to You; You know me inside and out,
You know every bone in my body
You know exactly how I was made, bit by bit,
how I was sculpted from nothing into something.
Like an open book, You watched me grow from conception to birth;
all the stages of my life were spread out before You,
The days of my life all prepared before I'd even lived one day.
Psalms 139:13-14 The Message Bible

Have you ever seen anyone cut the grass in a pair of royal blue stilettos? You may laugh as you imagine this scene and think, "This could be really entertaining!" But I know firsthand that it can be done. Stilettos are long, thin high-heeled shoes worn for a stylish, sleek look–not for comfort (or yard work for that matter). Although shoes can't tell a story, they may have a story to tell. Sometimes a memory is attached to a particular pair of shoes. My royal blue stilettos may have looked like an ordinary pair of pumps to someone else, but to me they were special because the story behind them was special.

Everyone loves a good story. We get lost in someone else's story. It captures our attention and warms our hearts or motivates us to become more than we have been. Did you ever consider that your story could matter? Within the pages of this book are stories of real people who come from many different walks of life. As you "step into their shoes," we hope that you will encounter the God Who was at work in their stories and will understand that His grace is also available to work in yours. We trust that your faith will increase with each turned page. We believe that through these stories, God will renew hope to the hopeless, faith to the discouraged, peace to the confused, and strength to the weary. We pray that many will obtain joy for their mourning, comfort for their loneliness, and healing for their brokenness.

Within the details of every story, you will see how God orchestrates good things out of seemingly hopeless situations:

an abused, pregnant runaway sleeping on the bathroom floor of a public park,
a business woman dealing with a husband's betrayal,
a young man plotting to kill a neighbor over drugs,
and a teenage girl making the difficult decision to place her baby for adoption.

As you read of a house built debt-free, yarn that reaches to Africa, and a fish story that proves that the moon doesn't have to be just right, you will become fully convinced of the incredible measures God will take to care for those closest to His heart: the abandoned, the fatherless, the widow, the orphan, the poor, and the broken. You will also see how God can manage the unexpected turns that we were never ready for.

Some of these stories will make you laugh, while others will tear at your very heart. You will be amazed as you read of the courage it took for a simple small-town hairdresser to step out and start a ministry from the ground up. You will be captivated by how God supplied funding through a community that had such an extravagant love for the hurting that they would go the extra distance to help because these girls and their stories matter.

As you read this book, you may remember various trials you have walked through that caused you to doubt that God even exists, but even that doubting is a part of your story. God created you, and your story matters to Him. Often we get so busy that we do not stop to recall the times that God has been faithful. I am sure He has been faithful to you even if you did not recognize it. By sharing these stories, we are recalling God's faithfulness in hopes that you will understand how much the God of this universe loves you.

Who would have ever thought that God would use a pair of blue stilettos to be a part of my journey? But He did. You will read about them in my story. As you do, I hope you realize that no matter what shoes you have walked in or where your steps have led you, *the story matters.*

Once upon a Time

Tammie's Story

As for me, God forbid I should boast about anything
except the cross of our Lord Jesus Christ.
Because of that cross, my interest in this world died long ago,
and the world's interest in me is also long dead.
What counts is whether we really have been changed into new
and different people.
Galatians 6:14-15 NLT

E veryone has a story, and I consider it a privilege to share parts of my story with you. But it is not my story that I want you as the reader to see, but who God is in my story. He is the most important part of my story. I believe life is like a puzzle, and if we allow the Lord to fulfill His purpose, He will fit each piece of that puzzle together in His perfect time. This is how the Lord began piecing together His purpose in my life....

Once upon a time, in a small rural town in South Carolina, I was born to a hardworking, loving couple. I was raised a country girl in a middle-class family. Surrounded by friends and extended family, I grew up playing outdoors on the twelve acres where our three-bedroom, ranch-style home was located. Playing in the woods by the creek and in the gullies and attending a nearby school about four miles from home were our only entertainment. Now I know when my brother and sisters read this, they are going to laugh and say, "When did you go to the gullies?" I really did play in the gullies, although I did love to dress up and will admit that I was the more "girly" one out of the three girls. (You will learn later on in another chapter how much I came to love fishing.)

My parents were hard workers at home and on the job. They instilled in the four of us that same work ethic that had been instilled in them by their parents. Every Saturday, we woke up early and spent the day cleaning the house, working in the garden, cutting grass–whatever needed to be done. I didn't like the yard work, so I did a lot of the cooking and cleaning in the house while my brother and sisters did the outdoor work.

My parents were not openly affectionate with lots of hugs and kisses, but they showed their love by the way that they nurtured us and provided a strong sense of safety and security. We just knew we were loved; there was never a question about it. They never yelled or fussed. They treated us with respect and expected respect from us as well. They taught us right from wrong, corrected us in love, and expected us to do our best at whatever we did. I am thankful for this legacy that was handed down to us, and I continue to instill these values into my children and grandchildren.

Living in the "Bible belt" meant that we attended church regularly, so my parents took me to Sharon Methodist Church during my childhood years. When we were children, we would pray every night before going to bed. One of my sisters or I would say, "Who's gonna pray?" Then another would pray our traditional prayer: "Now I lay me down to sleep..." I always felt that God was by my side, but at the time, I didn't know anything about having a personal relationship with Him. Now that I know Him in a more personal way, I realize that He was there all the time, and He wanted me to know more about Him and how much He cared for and loved me. The truth of the matter is that He loves each one of us because He created us to be in relationship with Him.

Later, in my teen years, when some of our extended family changed membership to another church, we followed them and went into town to Grace United Methodist Church. There I met a Sunday school teacher named Janice who seemed different from the other teachers. Looking back, I realize that the Lord was opening my eyes that I may see–giving sight to the blind (Isaiah 61:2, Luke 4:18). I had been in church, but I had never asked Jesus to forgive me of my sins and come into my heart. Being under Janice's teaching and prayers, I came to realize that I was a sinner who needed a Savior and that Jesus had died for me. That seed was planted, and it wasn't long before I found myself sitting on my bed, raising my hands to heaven and praying to Him.

Now the real journey would begin, and I would start learning things that only the Word of God and the Holy Spirit could teach me. I was about to enter into situations and circumstances that would forever change not only my life but also the lives of many others in the future. Here I was–a teenager who had been in church all my life. Although I had heard all the Bible stories, none of them had really stuck with me, and I had not had any "God stories" of my own. For me, it was not until I had first-hand experiences with the Lord that I really began to learn His Word, and it began to make sense to me.

I had always tried to be a "good girl." This for me meant that I shouldn't smoke, drink, curse, lie or have sex outside of marriage, and I should respect my parents. At the time, I had no idea that most of these were godly principles. When I say this, I don't mean to make it sound as though my parents or Sunday school teachers did not teach me anything. It was simply the fact that, at this time in my life, God was beginning to reveal to me His ways found in His Word. My eyes were finally beginning to open to the truth, and He was giving me a fresh new pair of lenses for me to see clearly what His Word truly meant and how it applied to my life!

Jesus said, "I am the gate. Those who come in through Me will be saved. Wherever they go, they will find green pastures. The thief's purpose is to steal and kill and destroy. My purpose is to give life in all its fullness" (John 10:9-10 NLT). However, for me, finding the green pastures would come later because soon I would choose to listen to the thief (Satan) who comes to steal. The enemy did not like it that I had given my life to the Lord; his plan of attack, as it has from the beginning, involved temptation. Here I was–a new believer, still a baby in my faith and relationship with Christ. I was trying to be good, but in Luke 18:19 it says, "No one is good except God alone" (NIV). It is only through Him and by our faith in Him that any good dwells within us. Through this, I realized that being so-called "good" wouldn't get me into heaven nor keep me from sinning. You see, I was what you call a weak-willed woman. Although I was not aware that I was weak, the enemy knew my weakness, and he knew the areas in my life in which he could tempt me.

I was a freshman in high school, working at our family-owned restaurant. Like most teenage girls, I had dreams of what I wanted to do with my life. I dreamed of becoming a hair stylist, but my biggest dream was to get married and have a family one day. I dreamed of having two children–a boy and then a girl. I had more than my share of crushes on guys and had dated many of them. Things changed, however, when soon after accepting the Lord into my life, I fell in love with a guy who swept me off my feet. David was four years older than I was. He had a job, and he bought me nice gifts and told me how pretty I was. He was also very good-looking, and all the other girls thought so too, which probably made me like him even more. I was just sixteen and thought I knew what love was, but I didn't have a clue. I guess you could say he became a distraction for me. We dated throughout my high school years. For the most part, my life revolved around him. I was still going to church, and I was even praying for him to become a Christian too. He told me he had accepted the Lord, and it sounded like he had had a real encounter with God. *(Even as I write this today, my prayer is that he is experiencing a personal relationship with Jesus. I know that God writes the final chapter to everyone's story. When we accept Him, it is as if He places a seal of approval on us (2 Corinthians 1:21-22), and He doesn't abandon His children).* Although I was still trying to be that "good" girl, I gave in to David's pressure and entered into a sexual relationship with him. Later, he gave me an engagement ring, and we talked about getting married and me going on to a technical school after I graduated. However, plans change sometimes because of our own choices.

During my senior year, I would go to school the first half of the day and work the rest of the day. Often, I would stop over at my uncle's house for lunch before going to work. One day, I was there eating vegetable soup, when my mother called and said, "I was hoping I would find you there. I'm about to be on my lunch break, and I'm coming to pick you up." When I asked, "But why, Mama?" she said, "You're going to the doctor today." In the car, I asked again, "Mama, why am I going to the doctor?" She replied, "Somebody told me you were pregnant, and we are going to the doctor to find out for sure." I didn't think I could be pregnant; I had no symptoms that I was aware of. The only thing I had noticed was that my belly was a little hard. Puzzled, I asked Mama how I could be pregnant when I was still having a monthly cycle. She responded, "I don't know, but we are going to find out TODAY." Sitting in the car, I felt an overwhelming dread smother me into silence. I knew that, pregnant or not, my sin had come to the light.

Shock and disbelief numbed my senses when the words, "Young lady, you are about to have a baby," came out of the doctor's mouth. His next words sent a wave of shock down my spine, when he announced, "You are six months pregnant." My world had just turned upside down in the worst sort of way. My parents were in shock as well. When the truth came out into the open, I was ashamed and embarrassed. Some people had looked up to me as a role model because I was a "good girl." Now, people talked about me and looked at me with scorn. I usually put up a front and acted like it didn't bother me, but deep down inside, it really did. I knew I had disappointed many people—including God. I stopped attending church regularly because I no longer felt worthy.

This shame was another strategy the thief was using to steal from me; and I believed his lie. I believed the lie because I did not know the truth. The truth was (and still is) that it is His grace and His blood that washes and cleanses us from our sins and that He is the one who gives us His righteousness and makes us worthy to wear His name. I John 1:9 says, "If we confess our sins, He is faithful and just to forgive us our sins and to cleanse us from all unrighteousness" (KJV). And Titus 3:3-6 says, "At one time we too were foolish, disobedient, deceived and enslaved by all kinds of passions and pleasures. We lived in malice and envy, being hated and hating one another. But when the kindness and love of God our Savior appeared, He saved us, not because of righteous things we had done, but because of His mercy. He saved us through the washing of rebirth and renewal by the Holy Spirit, whom He poured out on us generously through Jesus Christ our Savior" (NIV).

At any age, it is not an easy thing for a single woman to be dealing with an unplanned pregnancy; it is even harder for an eighteen-year-old who is still in high school. It was a very difficult and confusing time for me. I was teased by classmates and heard all sorts of bad advice. One person advised me to have an abortion. Even the teachers tore me down with their attitudes and looks. I did, however, have one teacher who encouraged me during the remaining months of school as I was preparing to graduate and trying to figure out what I was going to do. I knew that parenting was the only option I would ever consider, but I had a million questions running through my head every minute: "Where will I live?" "Who will support me?" "Should we get married now or wait?" "If we do, where will we live?" "What about graduating from high school and my dream of becoming a beautician?"

My dad called a family meeting to discuss my pregnancy. He told David, "You can marry her if you want to, but you do not have to marry her just because she is pregnant. We can take care of her and the baby." My daddy was protective of me and wanted to be sure that I was going to be loved and not mistreated. David still wanted to marry me, so we decided to get married sooner than we had planned—one month before I gave birth to my first child—a precious baby boy we named Stewart. It is amazing how quickly the shame and embarrassment faded away after I looked into that child's face for the very first time! It's true that a baby changes everything. They melt your heart, and it is never the same again.

We didn't have a house to live in, and there was no room at my parents' house because my brother and one sister were still at home, so David and I moved in with my grandparents. After a couple of months in their house, we rented a couple of places until we found a piece of land to rent and purchased a singlewide trailer to put on it.

Soon after we married, I saw a different side of David that I had not known before. What had seemed to be my dreams coming true soon became a nightmare that I wished I could wake up from. This was not the way I had wanted my story to go; it was not at all what I had planned or hoped for. I will not go into the details of this nightmare, but I will say that, almost one year after the birth of my second child, Kristi, the beautiful little girl that I had always dreamed of, I packed up our belongings and left. Having nowhere else to go and no support, my children and I moved back into my parents' home.

The decision to take my two young children and leave my home and husband was one of the hardest decisions I have ever made in my life. I never would have imagined that my life would wind up on such a devastating path. And I would have never thought that I would end up getting a divorce, not in a million years. This wasn't part of my hopes and dreams. The stress and the heartache that wrenched my body were almost unbearable. Because I knew divorce was wrong, I struggled to try to make a bad situation work. The mental wrestling between what I felt I should do and what I knew I needed to do left me in emotional knots. So I kept seeking God—to know His will for my situation. Eventually, I knew that He was releasing me from the commitment that I had made. Finally, I was at peace with myself and more importantly, with God. Many years down the road, as my walk with the Lord grew more intimate, He was able to lead me to the place where I could forgive not only David but also myself.

Although that season in my life was extremely difficult, two precious blessings came out of the mistakes that I had made, and these blessings are what I treasure. First, I experienced the most amazing love and support from my wonderful parents, and second, I was blessed with the precious son and wonderful daughter I had always wanted. I know the Lord doesn't make mistakes. And I believe in my heart that when these children were created, He said, "Well done." He was proud of His workmanship (Ephesians 2:10), and so was I. Do I believe I sinned? Yes! And I have been forgiven, and the Lord continues to take my mess and use it for His message. When God put these two pieces of the puzzle in place, He knew what He was doing, and I am forever thankful for my wonderful son and amazing daughter.

A New Chapter

We lived with my parents, and although they did help me a lot, I still took responsibility for my children as much as possible. Working at our family-owned restaurant, I barely had enough money to cover paying for day care, food, clothes, and gas to get back and forth. While I was thankful for my parents' allowing us to stay with them, I still felt a strong need to be in a home of our own. So I went to the unemployment office to find a better-paying job that hopefully would have benefits. There was one job opening that the clerk felt was right for me; it was an office job at a local clothing manufacturer. I had no skill or training in that area, but even while thinking to myself how crazy I was to even apply, I applied anyway; and surprisingly, I got the job. I didn't realize it then, but that was God's favor on me because He knew the plans that He had for me (Jeremiah 29:11). With this job came better pay and benefits—benefits that I really needed as a single mother.

With no skill, I had to be trained to do everything in my job description. Sandra, my office manager, trained me to do payroll, calculate production sheets, and order lining for shirts. She even taught me how to handle orders and business calls over the phone. Talking on the phone intimidated me, but because the job required it, I had to overcome this fear. Things were beginning to improve for me. Soon, I would be able to support myself and my children in a home of our own.

Once again, God had different plans. Sandra came up to me one day and said, "I know someone who wants to meet you." I said, "OK, who?" When she said, "It's my husband's cousin—John Wayne," I didn't believe her. I said, "John Wayne! He is stuck up! He doesn't even speak to me when he sees me." He regularly ate at our family restaurant where I would wait on him. This was the impression I had gotten of him when he dined there. John Wayne had grown up in the same community that I was raised in, but because he was thirteen years older than me, I just knew him in passing. At the time, I didn't know much more than this about him. I really did not know that he had a reputation for being a little on the wild side. Known around town as "The Duke," he often got into trouble when he would drink. Although I did not know enough about him to date him, I eventually agreed to at least meet him. What had caused John Wayne to want to date me in the first place was an encounter he had with the Lord. He was awakened one night from a dead sleep; he sat straight up in bed and clearly heard the words, "I've got a better life for you." After this experience, he told Sandra that he was looking for a "nice good girl." He needed to make some changes in his life and this was a good place to start. Sandra immediately said, "I know just the one for you, John Wayne, and she works in my office."

I did agree to go to watch the Super Bowl game at her house and meet him; however, after what I had been through, I was not at all interested in having a serious relationship. After all the hurts and disappointments I had gone through, I had put up walls that I hoped no man could break through. Many times after I first met him, he would ask me for a date, but I would respond by saying, "I don't know if I can find a sitter." He would reply, "That's okay with me; the babies are going with us." For this very reason, he soon became special not only to me but to my parents as well. When a single mom hears these words each time she is asked on a date, that tells you something is pretty special about that man. It makes him stand out. For a while, we dated each other while still dating other people because I wasn't planning to get serious with anyone, and he was still in an on-again, off-again relationship. Our dates always included my children, and on the weekends, his three sons from his first marriage would join us as well. He would have us over to his house and cook for us, and I would have him over to my parents' house. We didn't really do much going out on formal dates. Cautiously, I began to care about this man because of his kindness and because he cared for and loved both me and my children.

Although John Wayne and I were dating quite regularly now, the thought of marrying him had never really crossed my mind. I had never heard the philosophy that you shouldn't date someone you wouldn't consider marrying. But as time went by, this hard working man who wanted to protect and provide for me and my children slowly tore down my defenses. I cannot say exactly when it happened, but I fell in love with John Wayne.

I found out later from John Wayne's tales that this is not how it happened with him. To this day, his story of how he fell in love with me has always been a favorite family joke. The story goes this way: I stole John Wayne's heart when one day, while he and his father had gone fishing, I planned a special surprise for him. I knew they would be gone throughout the evening, so my plan was to get off work and surprise him by having his grass cut by the time he got back home. Yes, that meant that I would be the one cutting the grass! He did not have a riding lawn mower, so I was planning to use the push mower. It was 3:15 on a Friday afternoon when I clocked out from my job, still dressed in my nice outfit and a pair of royal blue stiletto pumps. His house was only about two miles from work, so I decided to go straight over there and get the grass cut before time to pick up the children from daycare. It would have taken me too long to drive several miles into the country to go home and change first, so I just went on to his house like I was. Yes, I cut grass in those royal blue stiletto "shoes" that I had worn to work. I thought nothing about it because I wore high heels like that every day. But, when John Wayne and his father returned home earlier than expected from fishing, he sure thought something of it! As he drove up into the yard and saw me mowing grass in high heels, he told his father, "I am going to marry that girl. Anyone that can cut grass and aerate the yard at the same time is the kind of woman I want!" Although we know they did not really make John Wayne decide to marry me, those blue high-heeled shoes were and always will be a part of our story.

I was oblivious of the effect that me and my blue high heels had on John Wayne, and as the days wore on, I continued to steadily work and save money towards my goal of buying a house for me and my children. Finally, my finances were looking better, and I felt I was ready to buy a house for me, Stewart, and Kristi. Although my daddy wanted me to stay with them so that he could protect us, I was determined to have a place of my own. I applied for an FHA loan and soon got the news that they had approved my loan. I was so excited! I called John Wayne with the news, and his reply took me by surprise. He responded, "You don't need a loan. I have a house, and you don't need one because we're going to get married." My shocked response was, "Oh, really? You think so? I am not so sure about that." So this was the way John Wayne proposed to me. We didn't make any definite plans, but every once in a while, he would bring it up casually and ask, "When are we getting married?" One day, I responded, "I'm not going to move into this house until you change this kitchen." His kitchen was old, with outdated colors of avocado green and harvest gold, and I hated the dark cabinets. He said, "All right, tell me what you want," and with that, he went and got a crow bar and started tearing cabinets out.

We married on April 7th, at Grace United Methodist Church. It was a small ceremony with just close friends and family. When we married, John Wayne had already adopted my children in his heart, but a couple of years later, he adopted them legally, and they took on his last name. My story was beginning to look somewhat like I had always hoped, although, as with any marriage, we had a quite a few obstacles to work through. Trying to blend two families always has its own challenges, but through the years, I adopted his boys, Johnny, Shannon, and Andy, into my heart as well. We continued to work through different issues and trials the best we knew how on our own. I worked at the local plant another three years and then went on to pursue my dream of becoming a licensed cosmetologist.

Over the coming years, we became a regular family with a normal busy routine. We worked, came home, fed the children, did homework, went to bed, enjoyed our weekends with all five children, got up and did it all over again. In that sort of busyness, God sometimes has to sneak in a few circumstances to prod you into the direction of what He had planned for you all along. This time, He used our daughter, Kristi. Kristi was struggling a little in school. We had heard that a nearby Christian school could give her the one-on-one attention that she needed in order to succeed academically; so in her third-grade year, we transferred her to this school. We thought we were sending her there to help her do better in school, but God knew the real reason we moved her there. Kristi began to learn God's Word and would come home and preach it to us. She had a new sermon to share with us every day. If she caught anyone in a "little white lie," she would surely correct that family member. One of the things she learned during the five years she was there was that a fetus is not just tissue; it is God's creation, a living human being. She realized that it should not be in man's hands to decide when to take that human being's life. She would tell us what she had learned about the life of an unborn baby. Psalm 139:13-14 is one of the clearest Scriptures on the unborn: "For You formed my inward parts; You covered me in my mother's womb. I will praise You, for I am fearfully and wonderfully made" (NKJV). We started to wonder, "What is God doing with this issue, and why would it become a topic of discussion quite frequently in our home over the dinner table?" At this point in our lives, we did not really read the Bible too often, and so our eyes had never been open to this truth. Up until then, we believed that everyone should get to choose for themselves. Although everyone does choose for themselves, we started to see that God had a plan for the infant in the womb.

Heart Surgery

Over time, we learned that our son, Stewart had some major health issues with his heart. At this point, the Lord led us to change churches (again because of Kristi's involvement with GCS). We moved to Calvary Chapel where John Wayne and I would learn that being a Christian was more than going to church; it was about a relationship. The heart surgery would soon begin. Not only would

our son Stewart begin going through repeated physical heart surgeries, but also God would begin spiritual heart surgery on both
John Wayne and myself, cutting away things that were not desir-
able to Him and allowing Him to build us up in ways that would
equip us to serve Him. He got us on our knees and taught us we
were not in control of anything. He turned us upside down so that
we could be right side up. We learned our only hope and peace was
through Christ alone. Through this spiritual surgery, He showed us
how to rely on and trust Him and to thank Him for the gift of faith,
which increased in measures day by day. We realized that we were
rendered helpless in the face of our son's condition; however, we
became empowered to simply know that God had Stewart in His
hands. It was at this point that God's deep, abiding peace seeped
slowly into our hearts.

Stewart underwent three heart surgeries that were unsuc-
cessful. Individuals and church congregations everywhere were
praying for him. The Lord placed Stewart on many people's hearts.
Someone told me that we should have Joe Hill pray for Stewart. (Joe
Hill teaches Sunday school at a local Baptist church and is known for
his gift of praying for others. The Bible tells about different people
having different gifts (I Corinthians 12:7-11). Joe has many spiritual
gifts, and God uses him greatly to touch many lives. I didn't know
Joe Hill at the time, so I let it go. Then another person mentioned
it to me as well, and I began to wonder if this was God's leading. A
few days later, a customer who knew our situation came into the
beauty shop. She had just come from a prayer meeting where Joe
Hill had prayed for her. He had said that she would have a special
assignment from God that day. Then she told me, "I feel like I'm
supposed to tell you to have Joe Hill pray for Stewart."

This happened two days before Stewart was scheduled to have
heart surgery at Duke University in North Carolina, and I had been
thinking about Joe Hill all day, wondering if I should take Stewart
to him for prayer. Stewart had already made it crystal clear that he
had no intention of going to see a "special man" to pray for him; his
church was praying for him, and he had gone before the elders and
had them pray for him as the Bible says to do (James 5:14). For him,
that was good enough. After this final confirmation, though, I knew

that this was God's plan. I arranged to go and stand in for Stewart since he did not want to go; so I called John Wayne and told him my plans of going for prayer after I got off from work. When I arrived home from work, I was surprised to see that John Wayne, Kristi, and Stewart were ready and waiting to go with me to the prayer service.

That night, God used Joe Hill in an amazing way to speak to all of us about our deepest concerns. Not only did the Lord do amazing things for our son's heart, but He changed my heart as well. I saw another facet of God's character through that free pair of "spiritual" lenses that He had given me early on. I realized how much He really cared about me and that He knew everything that concerned me. Joe prayed aloud every prayer that I had secretly been praying for my family; it was as if he was reading it off a piece of paper. He also prayed about my past—that I would be healed from the hurt in my teenage years so that God could use me. Rivers of tears flowed from the very depths of my inmost being. God healed my broken heart, and my life has never been the same.

A New Dream

Until this moment, I had silently carried the weight of my past. Even though my family had been supportive through it all, my teen pregnancy and my divorce both had always been a silent issue that we never openly discussed. At the time, these things just did not happen too often in the south. However, a few weeks after Joe Hill prayed for me, my mama called me and asked me to lunch. I will never forget that day. It was the first time since giving birth to Stewart that we actually talked about what had happened to me. She asked me if I would speak with a girl who was working with her. The girl was eighteen and pregnant and needed someone to talk to, but Mama did not know what to say to her and knew that I would be the one who could possibly help her and encourage her. It was then that I realized that God could use what I had been through to help others and that I could minister to others with the same comfort I had received (2 Corinthians 1:4). From this point on, the Lord began to open doors for me to reach out and offer hope to others in similar situations.

I met with this eighteen-year-old girl, prayed with her, and took her to the local crisis pregnancy center for them to counsel her. They gave her videos to take home for her parents to view. She wanted to give life to her baby, but her parents were not in agreement. They forced her to have an abortion. Stumped by this turn of events, I cried out to God, "Why? How could this happen? I thought You set this up for me to help this girl!" Since I had prayed with this girl and thought this was such a God-thing, I had felt that her parents would come around as well. At the time, I did not realize this was another piece of the puzzle that would one day be put into place. A few years after the ministry of A Place for Us was established, while cleaning out a drawer, I came across a notebook where I had written Scriptures and a message from the Lord. It said that many times in life, we cannot see the whole picture. The abortion this girl had was not His will; however, He does not force people to do His will. It is a choice, but prayers that we prayed, and my part in this would not be in vain. He was doing a work in my heart that I might understand His heart. It was not about me but about Him, and in time, I would understand. I realize now that this experience was pivotal in changing my perspective on abortion. I had thought abortion was just a personal decision that I should not interfere with. I did not understand how life is from God and how His heart breaks when we take it into our own hands and end it.*

Shortly after this encounter, another girl crossed my path. This time, it was through my husband; a friend of his had a sixteen-year-old daughter who was pregnant and needed some guidance. We were like most typical families: working, going to church, playing ball, paying bills, and enjoying our everyday lives. We weren't really taking time out to realize there were hurting people all around us. Once again, God interrupted what I thought my life should look like. I took this young girl to the crisis pregnancy center for counseling. The counselors there felt strongly that she needed to be removed from her home situation. The family was angry and hurt and wanted her to have an abortion. This suggestion led me to go and ask several churches if anyone would be willing to take her into their home, but I couldn't find anyone who was willing to do this for her. So I sent out prayer requests that we would be able to find a place for her as we searched for a safe home. Sadly, we discovered that there were not many maternity homes in South Carolina. Later, this girl was able to go to a Christian maternity home in the lower part of South Carolina. Girls who went there were provided with more than food and shelter; they were also taught life skills and Biblical principles.

I was able to make a trip down to visit her. While there, I met a fourteen-year-old girl who had been raped by her stepfather, and she was there because she wanted to give life to her baby. Yet she did not want her stepbrother to know what his father had done to her. The Lord used her story to grip my heart and capture my attention. I traveled back home alone that day. I say I was alone, but I don't think I had ever experienced the Lord's presence so strongly before. As I listened to Christian radio stations on the way home, every song that played and every speaker that aired that day related to the thoughts that were going through my mind as I traveled. Because of this encounter, I realized for the first time in my life that there were girls in this position who didn't have family or a support system and still had to make a difficult decision of what to do about their pregnancy. I saw that it was our responsibility as the church to offer a safe place for them. God was calling me to start a home that would be a refuge for these young girls. He showed me later in Psalm 18:18-19 how these girls may feel: "They attacked me at a moment when I was weakest, but the Lord upheld me. He led me to a place of safety; He rescued me because He delights in me" (NLT).

Out of the Blue

While this burden continued to grow in my heart, God was still rearranging my life to get me in position for His purpose. I sold my beauty shop and moved to Greenwood to join Edie's Hair and Nail Salon. Here the passion grew stronger. At first, I really did not want to share the dream with too many people. I still had not shared it with anyone in my family other than John Wayne, who also had felt the same burden; and the only people outside the family who knew about it were our prayer partners, Tommy and Bonnie. I wanted to know for sure that this was God's dream and not my own, so I was continually asking God to confirm His will and trusting Him that He would reveal it to me in His time. Late one night, I was sitting at the airport, waiting for my sister and her family to fly in from Hungary. It was getting later and later. A man kept coming up to my waiting area asking me if a certain plane had arrived. On his last trip, he sat down beside me. I had my head wrapped up in a jacket trying to nap but did not want to be rude, so I sat up and greeted him. He told me how tired he was and that he had just started a new job. Then he said that he had been working for DSS and would really miss that work. I listened as he talked about his job at DSS. Then I heard him say, "What South Carolina needs is more maternity homes." I thought I was going to fall out of my chair! I shared with him that I had asked God to speak clearly to me and to give me divine appointments that only He could set up. I am convinced that this was from God, and I would love to know who that gentleman was so that I could share with him how his obedience is making a difference in the lives of hurting young women and their unborn babies.

Confirmation from the Beauty Shop Chair

Along the way, as we prayed, expectantly waiting for His voice, little by little, He would show us who else to tell about this mission. It was at the beauty shop one day that I was prompted to share it with my customer Rayne. Not knowing why I should tell her or what role she might play in the ministry, I obeyed the Spirit's leading and told her what was on my heart to do. She listened intently and was very supportive of the idea. Still, month after month, I tried to delay starting this ministry, and with each hair appointment, Rayne would continue to ask me what I had done about what God was calling me to do. Sadly, I had to answer, "Nothing." At one appointment she said, "I have prayed and spoken with my husband about this, and he has given me his blessing to serve in keeping the books for the ministry free of charge. And I will help get it set up as a nonprofit." Through her connections, she was able to enlist the services of Peter, a local attorney who would soon handle the legal side of setting up the non-profit free of charge. Rayne started out serving on the board of directors but would eventually join Peter on the advisory board on which they both still serve today. Rayne also enlisted my son-in-law Geoff who, due to his position at a local bank, had a wealth of knowledge in finances. Geoff has served on either the board or the financial committee since the inception of the ministry.

Rayne also became instrumental in pulling together the very first organizational meeting to discuss opening a maternity home in the area. In April of 2001, this meeting brought together a diverse group of people all with the same heart for these girls: two pastors, a realtor, a financial advisor for a bank, and eight others. We had twelve people at that meeting, and many of those became members of the board of directors. Most are still involved in the ministry eleven years later.

After this first meeting, there were still many days I wanted to and even tried to say, "No." I just did not see how God could use me to do this work for him. See, I was just that little country girl who only went to high school and later went on to be a beautician. It doesn't take a lot of book sense to do hair, but to start a ministry, wouldn't it take someone smart and rich? Well, the Lord assured me through various divine appointments and many confirmations that it only takes a willing vessel.

Our Road Map for God's Journey

I truly believe that the best map for your life's journey is the Word of God. It has all the directions you will ever need. It will carry you on a journey. When it seems you don't know when or where to turn, it will direct you every time. It will relate to every situation you will ever face. It will never leave you wondering or hopeless. The Word says, "You will keep in perfect peace all who trust in You, all whose thoughts are fixed on You!" (Isaiah 26:3 NLT) When you are on the journey, and it gets hard, and you wonder if you heard Him correctly, guess what? He is always on time, and during the wait, His peace will surround you.

Enlarged Territory

As the Lord began to direct me in the work of building the ministry of A Place for Us, He daily continued to put the pieces of the puzzle together. At Edie's Hair Salon, today known as Tanglez, the Lord continued to bring people to my hairdresser chair that would be helpful in the founding of the maternity home. A dream conceived in my heart now slowly began to form until the full stages of labor and birth would bring it into reality. The stylists at Edie's published a cookbook and raised more than $16,000 for the ministry. Even today, these cookbooks are still being sold to support A Place for Us. Many of my co-workers and customers are still partners with the ministry. On this job, I schedule appointments, working customers in where there is time. I have learned, however, that God has His own schedule, and He delights in arranging appointments with the people He has already picked out to be part of His work. The Lord used a customer to teach me about His "divine appointments." Gwen Adams, a precious lady who has since gone to be with Jesus, brought in a book entitled *The Prayer of Jabez.* This book encourages Christians to pray and ask God to allow divine appointments in their lives. As I read this book, He began to do just that. People that I needed to call would just call me out of the blue or show up at the beauty shop. I also began to pray the prayer found in 1 Chronicles 4:10: "Oh that You would bless me indeed, and enlarge my territory, and that You would be with me and that You would keep me from evil, that I may not cause pain" (NKJV).

Here was a small-town country girl praying a huge prayer— a prayer for an enlarged territory. God didn't look at my education, my status as a divorced woman, my shame as a teenage pregnant girl, nor my qualifications. He simply looked at my heart. He saw that I was willing to do what He had called me to do. He reminded me that God doesn't call the qualified, but He would qualify the call which was inside of me. He was about to take my mess and turn it into a message that would bring hope and healing to others.

More Pieces to the Puzzle

There are so many more pieces to the puzzle of my life. Over the years, our family grew, and I became a grandmother of eight. From poor health to tragedy, through joy and grief, God has always brought His part of the story to light in the end (Romans 8:28, Psalm 34:18). We faced health issues with Stewart and Johnny. Later, we stood with Johnny and Cathy through several years of infertility until God finally answered their deepest cries with our miracle baby. We suffered the devastating loss of our son Shannon when he was killed in a truck accident at the age of twenty-seven. We were broken-hearted, shocked, and confused. Was God still good? We learned to trust and know that God IS still good, and we saw and experienced for ourselves His faithfulness. God is still good, and He is ALWAYS faithful!

Although there is so much I could have shared from many of these life stories, I am sharing only the stories that God used to birth this ministry. First, I had personally experienced much of what the girls we now serve face: teen pregnancy and the guilt, shame, and lost dreams that come with it, premature marriage because of pregnancy, and single motherhood through divorce. Second, I had personally experienced God's grace and forgiveness and the way He so lovingly takes our brokenness and turns it into something beautiful that He can use to touch someone else's life.

Your Story Matters

I am pretty sure if you are reading this book, there are pieces of the puzzle to your life that have not yet been put into place. But I promise that when you say, "Yes" to God, you will never be the same, and the picture will be a beautiful masterpiece that can only be put together by the Master of the Universe, the One Who created the heavens and earth and every living thing. He sees things in completion, and He wants you to share your story so that someone else might see Him too. What has God done for you? He has been there through every disappointment no matter what that might be or what it looks like. He can take what you went through and use it for good. My story was just the beginning of God opening the prison doors and setting the captives free, giving sight to the blind, healing the broken heart, and giving beauty for ashes. I experienced Isaiah 61 in my own life first, and I am forever thankful for the grace that He extended to me. Not every girl that ends up in my shoes has a loving family, or a "John Wayne" that comes along to help them through the hard places. But the great thing is a community of people have joined together to offer a place where healing can be found. I am thankful for the people who have allowed me to include them in my story. My prayer is that it will make a difference in someone else's life. If this ministry or this book changes one life for the good, then that one life may change ten thousand.

My name is Tammie...and my story matters.

*If you or someone you know has had an abortion or even considered abortion, you may be suffering from the effects of that decision. There is information and a prayer for healing in the back of this book for you.

The Inside Scoop

The Fish Story

Then He said, "Throw out your net on the right-hand side of the boat, and you'll get some!" So they did, and they couldn't haul in the net because there were so many fish in it.
John 21:6 NLT

N ow what would you think someone would do next to start up a ministry? Well, for me and John Wayne, we went fishing! John Wayne was an avid fisherman, and both he and I loved traveling down to Santee Cooper to go fishing for catfish. So on June 6, 2001, we headed down to Santee on a fishing trip that would soon turn into a mission. During this four-hour trip, I decided to use the time to read over several manuals I had received from a lady who had been running a maternity home for twenty-plus years. While studying, an idea suddenly hit me. I asked my husband, "Now, John Wayne, if God is going to do this—and He has to, because we don't have the resources, and we don't have a house—and if this is something that we are supposed to have in our community, then God is going to have to do it. Do you think we could sell tickets and have a fish fry?"

He said, "You can sell catfish, but you couldn't sell other fish."

While discussing this idea, John Wayne asked me just how many plates we would have to sell to raise enough money to begin. I quickly grabbed a piece of paper and jotted down some figures and came up with 250 plates. John Wayne exclaimed, "Two hundred and fifty plates! Who is going to catch all those fish, and better yet, who is going to cook them?"

I knew that I was probably looking for a miracle for both of those things to happen, but I was willing to step out in faith and give it a try. Still on the road, we called Tommy and Bonnie Boyd, who were great friends of ours and also powerful prayer partners. After we briefly shared the fish fry idea with them, we asked them to pray in agreement with us that we would catch an average of fifty fish a day. That way, we could host the fish fry and sell enough tickets to cover the start-up cost of the ministry. We felt that if this was something God wanted us to do, then we should not use our own money, for two simple reasons: One, our money would run out pretty quickly, and two, if this WAS a calling from God, then HE would send the provision.

We arrived at the lower lake of Santee around one o'clock that afternoon and stopped in at Harry's Fish Camp. Santee Cooper is a huge body of water with an upper lake and a lower lake with a canal running between them. John Wayne liked fishing in the lower lake because it was less challenging to stay anchored and less dangerous when the wind was blowing. I remember that it was a beautiful day, and I thought it would be just perfect for fishing. First, we pulled in to the store in order to check in and get our room key. I was not expecting to engage in a conversation with Mike, the owner. Mike is a very busy man and doesn't usually have time for chit-chat when customers enter the store. However, that day, even before he had time to look at our reservations, he asked, "How long are y'all going to be here?" I told him that our reservations were for a week. He nonchalantly said, "Well good, maybe you will catch some fish by the end of the week. No one is catching fish right now, but by the end of the week they should be biting."

"That is not good news," I replied.

He said, "The moon is not right for good fishing."

His advice could have burst my bubble like a needle puncturing a balloon, but I really believed this fish fry idea was from God; and I knew that, if it **was** from God, then the fish would bite **before** the end of the week. I just couldn't keep quiet. I told him that we were praying that we would catch fifty fish a day so that we could go home and have a fish fry to raise funds for starting a maternity home. The gruff fisherman half-heartedly chuckled and said, "Well, I hate to tell you, Ma'am, but if you are praying to catch fifty fish a day, your knees are going to be raw before you leave here."

"Well, why is that?"

He answered, "Because I told you—the moon is not right yet. Even the guides aren't catching."

The man's discouraging remarks didn't keep us from getting the boat unloaded and into the water. It was already getting late, and we wanted to start our mission. We unloaded the boat into the murky waters of the Santee and went out only about a hundred yards from the dock. We cast our rods and, to our sheer delight, caught forty-four fish in a five-hour time span. A rising storm forced us to stop fishing prematurely; otherwise, we would have caught more.

As we cleaned our fish, the other fishermen—one after another—arrived back at the camp. Bewildered, many stopped and stared, gawking at all of the huge catfish spilling out of our fifty-gallon cooler—each weighing anywhere from two to twenty-five pounds. The most any of them had caught was two to four fish, and they had been fishing all day. Some had even paid guides to help them locate the best fishing spots. Already, we were beginning to see our prayers answered.

The second morning, before heading out, we prayed, thanking the Lord for yesterday's catch and asking His blessing on the day's catch. We also asked that, if this maternity home was truly what He wanted for us, then He would cause us to not only catch our fifty fish for the day but to also make up the difference from yesterday's lack. He didn't just make up the difference; He doubled it! We caught a total of ninety-five fish that day. I had never been so tired in all my life. Reluctantly, we finally had to head back to the camp, but it wasn't because the fish had quit biting. The only reason that we had to quit was that we would never have finished cleaning all those fish before the fish shed closed that night. This was the day that I had to learn how to clean fish; otherwise, we never would have gotten the job done.

Our son Andy and his wife Valerie, along with Savannah, our first granddaughter, came to join us that night. The next day, the five of us went out and caught fifty-eight fish by 4:30 that afternoon. On the fourth day, we went out again and caught well over fifty fish. At one point, the other fishermen were following us, thinking that we had the inside "scoop" on where the fish were biting. Amused, we asked them why they were following us. They told us, "Mike said to follow you because you have a special connection."

To this, we replied, "You can have the same connection we have."

The interesting thing about that was, that even though they were following us, they still were not catching the miraculous number of fish that we were. The fact of the matter is that it really didn't have anything to do with us other than the fact that God had just found two people who were willing to pray and see exactly what God had up His sleeve.

To top it all, the owner of the fishing camp actually gave us fishing lure from his store—free of charge—just to see if we could catch fish on it. It did not take us long to realize that it wasn't about the spot nor about the fishing lure. God was in charge, and He wanted to see that a maternity home was started. Isn't it amazing the measures God will take to show His children how great and awesome He is and just how far He will go to prove His love for us and for those who have never felt or experienced His love?

The final count was an average of sixty-five fish per day—fifteen fish MORE than what we had asked or imagined (Ephesians 3:20). These fish were all so large that every one of them with the exception of four had to be filleted due to their size. Our coolers were full and running over. In fact, we had to return home early because we didn't have enough room to bring back any more fish. Needless to say, by the end of the week, when "the moon WAS right," WE were NOT fishing.

"Who's Gonna Cook All Those Fish?"

The fish were caught. Now John Wayne was concerned about how in the world he would be able to cook all of these fish. God, however, had already worked out those details. After arriving home from the fishing trip, Valerie went back to work and told her co-workers our amazing fish story. She told of the moon not being right and the prayers and the daily catch that exceeded our expectations and the bewildered fishermen and the faithful God Who confirmed His plan through a boat load of catfish. Dr. Kevin Rust, also an avid fisherman, overheard Valerie telling the story. Amazed by what he recognized as a miracle, he decided that he wanted to be a part of what God was doing through this fishing story. Later that week, he went to his church and shared with the men at South Main Baptist about this miraculous story. After they heard, they willingly volunteered to help with this event. Upon hearing this good news, John Wayne breathed a sigh of relief.

The date was set, and the tickets were sold. Hungry "supporters" would be arriving soon to enjoy their plates of fresh catfish, hushpuppies, fries, and coleslaw. It was time to start frying the fish. John Wayne arrived at Greenwood Christian School where the fish fry would be held. He knew that a few volunteers would be there to help with the cooking but was still a little unsure about this huge task before him. He was delightfully surprised when he watched truck after truck pull into the parking lot—each carrying a cooker. Dr. Rust and his friends had brought eight cookers. The fish were all cooked, and John Wayne never had to unload the cookers off his own truck.

God-Connections from the Beauty Shop Chair

Before we had the fish fry, I had another question in the back of my mind: "How are we going to pay for the other food and items we will need for the fish fry? How are we going to cover the cost of those things and still make a profit?" I had no need to worry because, as usual, God had it already figured out.

One day at the beauty shop, I was telling the fish story to my client, Gwen Adams. After hearing this amazing "God story," she pulled out her checkbook and wrote our first donation to the ministry. This money covered the cost of purchasing most of the other needed supplies for the event. Other people who learned about our need also gave to the cause, and our expenses for the fish fry were paid up front.* Also, as talk continued at the beauty shop, another customer was also intrigued by the story. She suggested that we host a silent auction during the fish fry. We loved that idea! So things were set into motion for a silent auction. Other clients at the beauty shop would hear about it and would donate items or gift certificates. They would tell their friends about it, and the friends would donate too. We received expensive jewelry, beauty and cosmetic baskets, and gift certificates to restaurants—all sorts of unbelievable merchandise to auction off. One of my customers convinced her husband to auction off a fishing trip through his guide service. John Wayne followed suit and donated a guided rabbit-hunting trip. These two trips ended up being the auction's biggest profit!

Another God-Connection

Although John Wayne had agreed to the rabbit hunt, he still had no idea where he could host it since we did not own any land.

Later, he was telling his friend Larry about the fish story, including everything from the fishing trip to the auction. When Larry heard about the rabbit hunt and the need for land to host it on, he volunteered the use of his farm for the rabbit hunt. Not only that, but he also offered to cook for the men and have skeet shooting available as well. John Wayne and I stood in awe of the goodness of God and how much he cares about the little things.

Because of the fish story, Larry got involved with this ministry. Later, he played a much-needed role in the building of the permanent home. He transported his heavy equipment all the way from Chapin, South Carolina, to clear the site for the home. Also, every year since that time, he has helped to underwrite our fundraising dinners.

250 Plates?

I know what you are wondering: "Did you sell 250 plates? Did you meet your goal? How much money did the fish fry and auction raise?" Well, we didn't keep a count of how many plates were sold that night, but the Greenwood Christian School cafeteria was totally packed with people enjoying these meals. I can tell you that the fish seemed to multiply—so much so, that we had enough left over to feed the men at the Faith Home, which is a local ministry that helps those who battle addictions. The total amount raised was just over $4,500—over three times the amount we had hoped for! With this money, we were able to design and order brochures and set up a checking account. The Lord's work had begun. He had shown us in more ways than one that the girls that we would one day help were very important to Him.

He sent us out on a boat to catch fish...
        ...now He would send us out to catch His vision...
            ...of saving real lives...
                ...all precious in His sight.

And that is no fish story!

This has been the pattern throughout the years. God will always prepare people's hearts to give, and when we host a fundraiser, all of our up-front expenses are already covered by the generosity of our gracious supporters and underwriters.

Turn the Radio On

Naming of A Place for Us

*Call to Me, and I will answer you. I'll tell you marvelous
and wondrous things that you could never figure out on your own.
Jeremiah 33:3 The Message Bible*

As the ministry continued to develop, next on the board's agenda was to find a name for the ministry. Bonnie Boyd, a member of our board and our prayer coordinator, called me one day and told me that she had heard the most beautiful song. While intently listening to the song lyrics, she thought about my vision for the ministry. She realized that we might be able to find a name for the ministry from some of the lyrics in that song. Bonnie was not quite sure about all the words, but thought it went something like, "There's a place for us where healing waters flow, where peace will come" and something about "a house filled with love." The song was "A Place for Us,"[1] sung and recorded by Kim Hill. As she shared some of the fragmented lyrics, I knew that I didn't even need to hear all the words. I told Bonnie, "That's it! 'A Place for Us.'" The name was perfect for the home that would shelter hurting young women and their babies. The words of the song were also quite fitting for what I felt the mission statement should include.

A Place for Us
Written by Jimmy Scott and Wayne Tester
Recorded and performed by Kim Hill

There's a place for us
Where healing waters flow
Where peace will come
And love will grow
By a river of compassion
There's a house filled with love
Somewhere in His perfect grace
There's a place for us

When the world outside turns hard and cold
And from your eyes the tears overflow
When a golden chance slips right through your hands
And you've built your dreams on shifting sands
When the road that lies ahead seems so hard to find

There's a place for us
Where healing waters flow
Where peace will come
And love will grow
By a river of compassion
There's a house filled with love
Somewhere in His perfect grace
There's a place for us

There's a tree of life, branches reaching high
By a stream of hope that never runs dry
There's a home where shelter can be found
If you walk on faith to that higher ground
Down the road that lies ahead
New life's waiting there

Years later, Sherri Lewis, the program coordinator, made arrangements for the residents, the house staff, and herself to attend a retreat at the Billy Graham Training Center at the Cove in the picturesque mountains of Asheville, North Carolina. Since she was new to the ministry, Sherri was not aware of how we had gotten our name. One day while talking to Lesa Jefferies, the program director, she mentioned the plans for the trip to the conference. When she said that a lady named Kim Hill would be leading worship, Lesa's eyes popped wide open. She went to her computer to see if it was the same Kim Hill who had sung the song "A Place for Us." To her great surprise, she found out that it was the same Kim Hill. They prepared a packet of information explaining the mission and vision of the ministry and mailed it to Kim, letting her know how much the song had impacted our ministry as it was being formed.

Soon, the time for the conference arrived. Two residents took the trip with Sherri and the other staff member. Kerri, one of the residents, was not a Christian. During the praise and worship, Kim felt led to sing a song that has been a favorite for many of our residents. It talks about Jesus holding us when we are afraid and lonely and about Him being our Prince of peace. While she sang, the Holy Spirit began to move and speak to Kerri's heart, and she ended up giving her life to the Lord that night. The next day, the girls decided to ask Kim Hill to sing at the fundraising banquet for A Place for Us Ministries. Kim agreed to prayerfully consider it. The Lord led her to accept our invitation, and she ministered at our banquet that same year. Of course, in the beginning, when this special song led us to our name, none of us had had any idea that one day Kim Hill herself would be singing "A Place for Us" at one of our fundraising banquets. That night, the One who had orchestrated every detail blanketed the place with His healing presence as Kim sang so powerfully. What a blessing it was for us to witness her heart for this ministry firsthand! She later returned and ministered at our "On the Heels of Hope" conference, a community-wide ladies' conference sponsored by A Place for Us Ministries.

Beauty for Ashes

With everything involved in starting a ministry, there were so many things to consider. However, it was a comfort to know that we were not the ones making the decisions. God was causing the pieces to come together. We were learning not to run ahead of Him but to wait on His perfect timing. We had the name. Now it was time to design an eye-catching brochure that would relay the mission and vision of A Place for Us Ministries. That would mean our brochure would need to have a guiding scripture for the ministry. This scripture would be foundational to everything we did as a ministry.

The board members planned to take two weeks to pray and seek the Lord about what our guiding scripture would be. After seeking the Lord daily, I woke up on the morning of the board meeting, still with no word from God. I prayed again that the Lord would show me the guiding scripture; I picked up a devotional entitled *Life in the Word* by Joyce Meyers. The devotion that I turned to was based on Isaiah 61: "Thousands of people have been hurt severely in their lives. They come from broken relationships or abusive backgrounds that are still producing bad fruit in their personalities. God wants to send the wind of the Holy Spirit into our lives (Acts 2:1-4) to blow away the ashes that are left from Satan's attempt to destroy us and to replace those ashes with beauty."[2]

When I read the devotional, I remembered the first time that I had really understood that particular passage of Scripture. I was on a fishing trip with John Wayne at Santee Cooper in the year 2000. This was one year before the Lord began to deal with me about the starting of this ministry. At that time, I not only understood that this was what Jesus had come to do, but I also realized that it was what Christians were called to do. That Scripture struck such a chord with me that I began to memorize some of the verses while I was on the fishing trip.

After reading the devotional that morning, I began to see that the Lord was speaking to me His plans for A Place for Us Ministries. Later the same day, while I was working at the beauty shop, one of my clients, Theresa Davis, shared a word from the Lord. She said, "This morning, when I got up, the Lord said that when I came to get my hair done today, I needed to tell you that you needed to look up Isaiah 61." She told me that she didn't really know what that meant but that God had said I would understand. This was all the confirmation I needed, realizing that this message from Isaiah 61 would indeed be our guiding scripture. (Theresa later became a board member for APFUM, and she still supports the ministry today.)

That evening, when the board meeting began, I was very excited about how clearly the Lord had shown me the guiding scripture that day, but I did not want to get ahead of God. Instead of speaking first, I allowed each of the other board members to take turns sharing what God had shown them. This was a very powerful moment in the history of A Place for Us, and I stood in awe as we went around the table and every single person in the room individually said, "Isaiah 61"..."Isaiah 61"..."Isaiah 61." The Lord had spoken, and His sheep had heard His voice. What an amazing confirmation of God's plan for the ministry!

Isaiah 61
The Spirit of the Sovereign LORD is on me,
because the LORD has anointed me
to proclaim good news to the poor.
He has sent me to bind up the brokenhearted,
to proclaim freedom for the captives
and release from darkness for the prisoners,
to proclaim the year of the LORD's favor
and the day of vengeance of our God,
to comfort all who mourn,
and provide for those who grieve in Zion—
to bestow on them
a crown of beauty instead of ashes,
the oil of joy instead of mourning,
and a garment of praise instead of a spirit of despair.
They will be called oaks of righteousness,
a planting of the LORD
for the display of His splendor.
They will rebuild the ancient ruins
and restore the places long devastated;
they will renew the ruined cities
that have been devastated for generations.

Strangers will shepherd your flocks;
foreigners will work your fields and vineyards.

And you will be called priests of the LORD,
you will be named ministers of our God.
You will feed on the wealth of nations,
and in their riches you will boast.

Instead of your shame
you will receive a double portion,
and instead of disgrace
you will rejoice in your inheritance.
And so you will inherit a double portion in your land,
and everlasting joy will be yours.

"For I, the LORD, love justice;
I hate robbery and wrongdoing.
In my faithfulness I will reward my people
and make an everlasting covenant with them
Their descendants will be known among the nations
and their offspring among the peoples.
All who see them will acknowledge
that they are a people the LORD has blessed."

I delight greatly in the LORD; my soul rejoices in my God.
For He has clothed me with garments of salvation
and arrayed me in a robe of His righteousness,
as a bridegroom adorns his head like a priest,
and as a bride adorns herself with her jewels.

For as the soil makes the sprout come up
and a garden causes seeds to grow,
so the Sovereign LORD will make righteousness
and praise spring up before all nations.(NIV)

God's desire for A Place for Us Ministries is and has always been to offer hope to these hurting girls—hope for today and hope for tomorrow. These powerful words of Isaiah 61 became our hope, planted not only in the hearts of seven founding board members but also in the hearts of future board members, staff, and volunteers. We want to see freedom for the captives, release for the prisoners, beauty for ashes, gladness instead of mourning, praise instead of despair, and joy instead of shame through the power of the Lord Jesus Christ for every person whose lives we are blessed to touch.

God Answers Knee Mail

The Furniture Story

*Your Father knows what you need
before you ask Him.
Matthew 6:8 NIV*

This is one of my favorite stories of the ministry. It shows how God provides—sometimes even before we need it. I believe that when He does this, it is just a sign of things to come to keep you going and believing for what He is calling you to do. After our very first opportunity to share the vision at a church, I left there thinking, "How will we ever build a home if we don't ask for money?"

But the Lord was saying to me, "You will not have to ask; I will. LET ME!" Just two days had passed when I got a call from Erin, an old high school acquaintance. Erin had heard the message and had found out that I worked at Edie's, so she called me there to ask if we could use some beds for the home. My first thought was, "Does she not realize we don't have a house?" I told her that eventually we would need beds, but we did not have a house and had no idea when we would.

Erin said, "I know, but you will need them, and the company I work for is looking for someone to donate six beds to. After I heard the presentation at my church, I thought you would need at least six beds."

I said, "Yes, we will be able to house six girls, as a matter of fact. Can you give me some time to locate a place to store them temporarily?"

The company Erin worked for had been housing employees but was now doing away with some of the apartments. We asked around, trying to find somewhere to store the beds. After I told the story to Alice, a customer at the beauty shop, she offered to let us use a small metal building behind her home. It would be our responsibility to move the beds. However, as I started the process of searching for a way to move them, Erin called to tell me that the beds were loaded, but the driver needed to know where to take them. As soon as I could hang up the phone, I called Alice about her building. It was very unusual that she did not answer at 8:30 a.m. I called the driver to tell him that we had a metal building, but I could not get in touch with Alice, and I didn't know where she lived or even how big the shed was. All I knew was that Alice had told me it would hold six beds. He let me know right quick that there was no need to wait for Alice because a metal shed that would hold six beds would not come close to storing everything the company was donating.

Surprised, I said, "What do you mean? That is all Erin mentioned to me–that they had six beds." He told me that we would not only be getting six beds, but the bedroom suites that matched, three den sets, three dinette sets, three washer and dryer sets–pretty much everything you could think of to set up a three-bedroom apartment times three. I could not believe what I was hearing! He informed me that it would take a large storage unit, and even that would be cutting it close.

I had heard everything he said, but I still could not wrap my mind around this unexpected blessing. It was overwhelming to see this come without asking. At the moment, however, I couldn't even think about that because one load of furniture was already on the truck, and the driver was waiting for directions to a storage unit. What was the wise thing to do in this situation? I did not have time to call all the board members and ask them to take a vote. I had two options. I could tell the driver we could not use the furniture because we did not have a storage building, or I could call storage companies and rent a storage building. The problem with the second option was that the only money available was what was left from the fish fry after we had paid for brochures. I couldn't help but wonder how long that money would last if we had to pay rent on a storage unit every month for who knows how many years. Only God knew how long it would be before we had a house. Then, in just a quick moment, the thought came to mind, "Call storage units." So I told the Lord how I felt, "Lord, I am confused right about now." The surprise donation had seemed to be a God thing, but He was going to have to do something quick or else I would soon believe other-wise. I went through the yellow pages, calling to get prices for large storage units. The answer with every call was $120.00 per month, and even if we could have afforded that, none were available. After each call, the thought would nag, "I just don't think we are going to be able to take this furniture." When I realized there were only two numbers left in the yellow pages, I remembered a billboard I had seen earlier in the week that said, "God answers knee mail quicker." I got on my knees and prayed, "Lord, if this furniture is for the ministry home, we need storage, and we need it quick." It seemed to me like hours had gone by because I knew the driver was still waiting for me to call back and give him directions. I called the next place, and out of desperation told the lady the whole story, yet she also said, "Sorry, we do not have a unit available either." Then she added, "But don't give up; something is going to come open."

I responded, "I am not going to give up; I have one more number to call." It may have been the first listing in the phone book, but for some reason, it was the very last number I called. A sweet lady, Ms. Roberta Dill, answered the phone. I told her why I was calling, and she said that she did have one available. I reluctantly asked, "Are yours $120.00 per month as well?"

She replied, "Yes, they are, but you can have it free of charge until the Lord builds this house."

"What? Wow! I can't believe what I am hearing! Are you sure?" was my response.

I had never met Roberta Dill, and to this day I stand amazed that this precious lady, who knew nothing about A Place for Us Ministries or Tammie Price, gave so willingly right on the spot. Her reply to my shock was, "Yes, I am sure. You can tell them to deliver it here." As always, God is on time, and He has connections I never would have dreamed possible.

After this amazing encounter, I got dressed, and went to the site of the apartments. Here was another God thing. I work part-time at the beauty shop, and this was supposed to be a workday for me, but for some strange reason, weeks before ever hearing anything about the furniture, I had marked it off in my appointment book as a day off. I didn't know why I was taking the day off, but God did. Like the scripture says, "I'm an open book to You; even from a distance, You know what I'm thinking. You know when I leave and when I get back; I'm never out of Your sight. You know everything I'm going to say before I start the first sentence. I look behind me and You're there, then up ahead and You're there, too, Your reassuring presence, coming and going. This is too much, too wonderful—I can't take it all in" (Psalm 139:2-6 MSG).

This last verse describes exactly how I felt when I arrived at the apartments to find others there with boxes and tape. They said,

"You need to pack everything; it is all going to the ministry you are starting." We packed items from three apartments, so every item came in threes. There were shower curtains, ironing boards, irons, dishes, pots and pans, microwaves, pot holders—everything you can imagine to set up house. We boxed them up and sent them, along with all the like-new furniture, to the storage unit graciously donated by Ms. Roberta and her husband. It stayed there rent-free for two years. After the two years, we were able to move it all into the 10,000 sq-foot warehouse of The Alcoves. In God's amazing timing, two weeks after we moved the furniture into the warehouse at The Alcoves, the same company called to see if we could use more furniture—six houses full! Needless to say, this time storage space was not an issue. By then, the permanent home was near completion. This second delivery provided the rest of what we needed to completely furnish the home. We were also able to sell some of the furniture to pay for some decorating at the home.

We had always hoped we would have matching furniture. From the three apartments, we did get three matching couches that could have worked. They were in very good condition, but the pattern on them was outdated. One day, a lady came into the store who wanted to know if she could bring in pictures of her sectional couch in hopes that she could sell it and give a percentage to the ministry. We did this sometimes with what we called floating space. It was a beautiful cream-colored leather couch with a lifetime warranty. We sold the ones we had and purchased the cream couch, which was a lot newer and would match nicely with the colors the decorator was planning to use at the permanent home.

With the home fully-furnished, we still have other pieces that we plan to use for transitional housing at some time in the near future. These cottages will accommodate residents who have completed the program, offering them safe, affordable housing while on their journey to becoming independent. The furniture story is just one of the many ways God provided to show us that He had a plan to build a home for girls in crisis.

Two Different Churches—Same Big God

Every step along the way, it has been the generous people in the community that God has used to show His faithfulness. Without giving people, this ministry would not be in existence. The heart of this community has been expressed in several facets and through many different avenues. Even beyond this community, people have given from their hearts.

Dale, a lady who owned a Bible and book store near Columbia, South Carolina, contacted our ministry out of the blue. She loves helping raise money for charities. Somehow, our opening for a houseparent position came up on her computer one day. Sensing that this might have come to her attention for a reason, she called to find out more about our ministry. Wanting to help, she printed off the information and placed it in her store in hopes that the right person would see it and apply for the job.

One day a truck driver came into her store and saw the information about A Place for Us. He said that he might be able to get some paper products from the company he worked for. Excited, she called to let me know. Though this plan fell through, it had given her an idea that she couldn't shake. She told some ladies from her church about A Place for Us, and they discussed ways to help once the home was open. Several of them came and toured the home while we were waiting to fill the houseparent position. Excited, they went back to their small church of about thirty-five and shared the A Place for Us vision with their congregation. Although small in number, they had large hearts. They decided to pray about how they could help. The trucker's idea must have made an impression because they decided to contact a local paper product company in Greenwood and set up a prepaid account. This way, when the house needs paper products, the house staff can go by and pick up what they need for the home. To this day, this church still pays for the paper products for the home. This special gift from a small church proves that no matter how small you are, God has a plan for your church and you can reach out to the needs of others.

Another church, which is very large, began several years ago to give three percent of their year-end surplus to A Place for Us.

The donation has always come in three separate checks. When the church started a building project, the pastor asked me to pray that the money would continue to come in to cover the extra expenses involved while still having enough left to give the usual amount to A Place for Us. Realizing that it would take a lot of money for this church to complete this very large building, I prayed for provision every time I passed that new building as it went up.

The first check we got from them that year was not as much as we had been getting, but it was still a blessing, and we were very grateful. A few weeks later, we received the second check, which almost tripled the first one. When the final check arrived, I could hardly believe it. The total of the three checks was only slightly less than their usual donation. This amount just happens to be the exact cost of our insurance for a year and just happens to come the exact month our insurance is due. Before this time, paying the insurance had often been a struggle for us, even while making payments monthly. Ever since God called this church to give three percent from their surplus at year's end, we have been able to pay our insurance up front every year.

This is exactly what the body of Christ is meant to do. When we all do our part, it completes God's plan for the church. I believe this is also a testament to the A Place for Us Board's decision to always tithe ten percent of everything that comes in. Some ask why a ministry would need to tithe. It is a biblical principal—one that God actually says we can test Him in (Malachi 3:10). This verse has been proven true time and time again as God has been faithful to supply our needs month after month, year after year.

It Will Be Provided

The Land Story

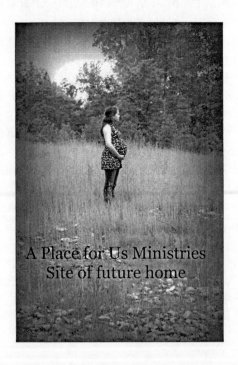

A Place for Us Ministries
Site of future home

Go through the camp and tell the people to get their provisions ready. In three days you will cross the Jordan River and take possession of the land the LORD your God is giving you.
Joshua 1:11 NLT

Time flew by, and on February 11, 2002, the board of directors for A Place for Us had a training seminar with Ann Pierson from Loving and Caring, a ministry which provides support and guidance to churches, pregnancy centers, and housing ministries. Ann had an abundance of experience in establishing and successfully running family-style maternity homes. She confirmed many thoughts and details that the board had been praying over. She also gave us valuable information concerning problems that would arise from purchasing an older home and the issues that would be counterproductive when trying to update it to meet certain codes. She suggested that we pursue looking for land so that we could build a home for the ministry. We all felt confident that the Lord was leading us in this direction. From the beginning, we had decided that we would like the home to be near the Abbeville/Greenwood county line so that we could serve both counties and their surrounding areas.

Just three days after this seminar, 4.4 acres of land, situated less than a mile from the county line, became available for purchase at the price of $14,900. Two things we had determined from the start were that we would always tithe 10% of the money that was contributed to A Place for Us and that we would not go into debt to build a home. If we were to purchase at the quoted price, there would only be approximately $75.00 left in our checking account. Depleting our account to this degree would create a problem with the finances of the ministry. One big problem would be not having the necessary funds to pay our secretary her weekly paycheck. This fact made our decision much more difficult.

We knew that we needed to act quickly on this, but no one felt comfortable making a decision unless every board member was present to vote. I also felt strongly that every board member should see the land in person before making a final decision. The problem was that one of our board members, Emily Allen, was out of town. We grappled with the question, "Should we move ahead with one board member out of town?" Finally, I called Emily and found out that it would be several days before she returned to town. However, she did say something else that gave me hope. She said, "I can tell you over the phone if we are supposed to purchase the land."

She went on to explain that she had been praying about the land, and the Lord had shown her that the property was located beside a creek. So her only question was, "Is there a creek on or beside the property?"

My answer was, "Yes! Yes! There is the most beautiful creek bordering the property!" God used Emily to confirm what the rest of the board had already been feeling about this land.

Another neat confirmation came when we learned the name of the person selling the land. Her name was Mariah. Donna Brounkowski, a board member, noticed a connection between Mariah's name and the story she had been studying as she prepared to teach Sunday school. The Lord had led her to Genesis 24, which tells how Abraham took his son Isaac to the top of Mt. Moriah where God had commanded him to offer Isaac as a sacrifice. When God saw his obedience and faith, he stopped Abraham and provided a ram for him to sacrifice instead. "So Abraham called that place *The LORD Will Provide*. And to this day, it is said, 'On the mountain of the LORD it will be provided'" (Genesis 22:14 NIV). We found that this scripture encouraged us that God would provide the finances to pay our secretary and to run the ministry. Not only that, but the story reminded us of the sacrifice Ms. Mariah was making to offer this land at such a reasonable price. It was very hard for her to sell off pieces of land that had been in her family for years. We honor her for this act of obedience.

We stepped out in faith and placed a contract on the land, closing the transaction on May 1, 2002. Many times, when you step out on faith, you wonder if you are out on a limb instead. You look around and wonder if you really heard from God and made the right decision—especially when your eyes only see the circumstances. The board discussed the fact that we still had to meet our payroll obligation for the secretary and felt that we should send out a letter to all our partners, letting them know that we were taking a step of faith to purchase this land. We extended an opportunity to anyone feeling called to sow into this endeavor with us to pray about an amount they were to give. In less than two weeks, over half the purchase price was back in our account. Here was another confirmation that we had stepped out in obedience to God when we purchased this property.

This piece of land was perfect. We did not have the house plan picked out yet, but we could already picture where the house would be situated. The 4.4 acre track was divided almost in half by the lay of the land. The house would one day sit on a knoll on the front two acres which had been cleared except for a few straggly trees. The backside of the remaining two acres gently sloped down to a spring-fed creek branch that was nestled among a variety of hardwood trees.

We had purchased the land, but we were a long way from having $385,000.00 to build the permanent home. Determined to stay debt free, we created a postcard to mail out to our partners. As a symbol of our faith, we took a picture of one of our birthmothers standing on the land. This picture became the cover of the post-card. We asked our prayer partners to agree that the Lord would supply every need for this permanent home to be built debt free. It was going to take a lot of faith and many people with giving hearts to construct a house built with LOVE.

Nothing We Asked For...But Everything We Had Hoped For

The Temporary Home Story

And if I go and prepare a place for you, I will come back and take you to be with me that you also may be where I am.
John 14:3 NIV

N estled among towering pines and overlooking the peaceful waters of Lake Greenwood, a small brick cottage would serve as our temporary home for two years. There had been many challenges involved in preparing this home, and through many amazing God stories, the project was completed. On February 23, 2003, a small gathering stood on the shore for the dedication ceremony. The board of directors along with friends, family members, local pastors, two future residents, and their families came to take part in dedicating the temporary home. As blessings were spoken and prayers were lifted up, our hearts' cries were that this ministry would not just be a place of shelter for these girls but that God would heal and transform their hearts and minds just as He had done with many of us standing there.

The temporary home was donated by Grace Community Church, one of many churches that supported A Place for Us Ministries. This church had envisioned purchasing this lake property to host retreats and special events designed not only for strengthening relationships within their church but also for facilitating outreach to the local community. Looking back on this blessing, we can see how the church had great plans for the use of this property, but, like all of us involved with A Place for Us, they did not see the whole picture and how their gift would fill a need that no one could have foreseen. Their providing this home would prove instrumental in the process of building the permanent home. After TWO years in this temporary home, as we began the grant-writing process, we discovered a very interesting stipulation. In order to be eligible for a matching grant of up to $150,000 for the building of a permanent home, the ministry needed to have been in operation for TWO years—the exact amount of time we were in the lake house before the church sold the property.

Back to the Beginning

I will have to back up to the beginning of how the temporary home came about. The text below is in the words of Donna Brounkowski, a member of our board and a realtor in Greenwood.

One Wednesday night, Tammie excitedly started telling me about an article that she had just read that day... about how Joyce Meyers Ministry had donated $150,000.00 to a maternity home in order to construct a new home. Tammie told me, "If God can do that there, I believe God can do that for us!" Now, I'll have to admit, Tammie's faith was way beyond mine at that moment. The very next morning, I received a phone call from one of the administrators at my church, and after the usual "How are you?" small talk, he asked me a very unusual question, "How would you like for me to make your day?"

I said, "Sure." He then explained to me that the church was about to purchase a piece of property on Lake Greenwood. On this peaceful peninsula were several cottages. The church wanted to know if the ministry would be interested in using one of them for our girls' home.

After I hung up I dialed Tammie and said "Are you sitting down?" She said "Do I need to be?"

To my "Yeah," she replied, "Don't tell me somebody wants to write us a check for $150,000.00 dollars!"

I said, "Not quite, but it's just as good."

A Place for Us accepted the offer and began getting the house ready to move in. There was a lot of red tape, but God specializes in breaking through red things...red tape...red seas...

It was really amazing how just the day before I had sat reading that article about the elaborate donation for a maternity home while tears flowed down my face, and I wept uncontrollably. I had felt the Lord was speaking to my heart, letting me know that He was about to prepare a way and send provision for a temporary home. Initially I thought someone was about to make a large monetary donation so that we would be able to purchase a home, but I soon realized that God had a different plan in mind. I have learned that when you are praying and asking God for things, you may not get anything you asked for, but what you get will be everything you hoped for and everything you need!

The church bought the property and allowed A Place for Us to use one of the cottages for the residents. The detached guest house was used for our houseparents' sleeping quarters since the other was too small to accommodate both the houseparents and the girls under one roof. However, their close proximity and an alarm system in the home provided security for the girls as they slept. It was a well-built home with brick exterior and wood-paneled interior from the floors to the walls, cabinets, and ceilings. Even this stained-wood interior fit into the plan because we would soon learn that it is very hard to get an old home approved as a group home through DHEC if it has any traces of lead-based paint. Of course, we had no problem with that requirement because this home had no paint.

The paint issue was just one of the many things that could have been an obstacle, but when God is able to move mountains, the things we would be facing would be no problem for Him! Another almost obstacle had to do with fire inspection policy. In order to pass fire inspection, there would have to be a fire hydrant within five hundred feet of the home. Wouldn't you know—a fire hydrant had recently been installed—five hundred feet from the house! God had provided before we ever knew the need. Later on down the road, He would teach us more about faith and fire hydrants when we were building the permanent home.

Next, we found out that we would need to provide the fire marshal with a floor plan of this house—another state requirement for opening a residential home for girls. With this being a fifty-year-old retreat house whose original owners had closed down most of their businesses long ago, the chances of finding the plan were next to impossible. However, someone connected us with Brian, a former employee of this business, who had access to keys to the property. He had never heard of A Place for Us Ministries but was willing to do what he could to find the floor plan. Knowing that God had connected us with this humble, quiet man, we were baffled when he did not find it. Then, we were amazed to learn that he was an engineer. As an engineer, he could draw us a floor plan and could do so within a few weeks.

Time was of the essence because we had already received desperate calls from parents of a sixteen-year-old from Seneca and parents of a fourteen-year-old from Spartanburg who were both dealing with unplanned pregnancies and needed our shelter, help, and support. The only problem was that it would cost us thousands of dollars for him to draw up these plans—money that the ministry did not have at the time. However, Brian graciously provided his service free of charge. (From the very beginning, the board of directors had decided that we would not ask people to do things free of charge; instead, we would present the need and allow the Lord to show them what they were to do.) In this case as well, we did not ask Brian to do any of this for free; he just offered his service out of the goodness of his heart. It seemed as though he was an angel who came out of nowhere at just the right time. To this day, each time I run into Brain, he wants to know how things are going with the ministry.

Amazing things continued to happen as we watched God's provisions come in. The security system mentioned earlier not only served for security purposes but was also another requirement from the fire marshal. We needed this system in order to meet the fire code. We had to install a fire system and heat sensors in every room, and they had to be monitored since the house was not built to code. The estimate originally given to the ministry to install the fire system was $4,500. Once again, the money was not there for this unexpected expense. The board of directors spent the weekend praying about it, and by Wednesday, $2,800 had been donated by several different individuals who had heard of our need and had gladly given to the cause. The security system company then lowered the price to $3,500, and more donations came in to completely cover the cost.

We also realized just days before opening the home that we did not have towels for the bathrooms. The next day, Luster, a customer at Edie's, brought in a bag of towels. She had been shopping that weekend and noticed that the towels were on sale. She immediately thought of the ministry and, on the spur of the moment, decided to buy them for us. Unlike with the security system, we had not taken time to send out a prayer request; no one had known our need except the One who prompted Luster to buy those towels. Shortly after this special delivery, another customer came in and noticed the bag of towels lying there. Curious, she asked about them. As I told her the story, she spoke up and said that she worked for a towel plant and would ask if they would be able to donate some towels as well. She later came and delivered enough white towels to fill the entire linen closet. Day after day, many other little details came together in just the same way.

A Place Called Home

The rustic little home with the partial wrap-around screened porch had a small kitchen and dining area leading to a den with a huge window overlooking the lake. The two large bedrooms provided adequate space to house two double beds and matching nightstands, which had been donated. The shared bathroom between the two rooms would serve our needs. Although we were so thankful to have a donated home which would soon house four residents, it still lacked something. It lacked the color that it needed to make the place seem more like a home. Gina, another of my salon customers was a seamstress. One day, while I was cutting her hair, we were discussing how God had provided a home for the ministry. As I described the home, Gina asked if we would like her to make curtains. I thought that was wonderful but knew that we did not have money to spend on fabric for curtains. Shortly after Gina's appointment, Lynn, a professional seamstress, came in for her appointment. After I told her about Gina offering to make the drapes, she got on board and decided to use her connections to get us the fabric for the drapes. Because of her efforts, Sara's Fabrics, a fabric store in Abbeville, gladly donated the fabric. This addition to the den, dining room, and kitchen made the house seem more like a home.

Having this fabric and drapes donated wasn't the end of how the true Decorator demonstrated how much He cared even about every little detail of the home. One day before our first two girls came through our doors, several board members commented that we needed den furniture that would be comfortable. Within a few short days, we received a call from someone wanting to know if we needed a sectional couch. We held our breath as the would-be donor began to describe the couch. (We were hoping that the kind donor was not getting rid of an old harvest-gold and dingy-orange plaid couch from the 1960's.) Much to our surprise, the sectional couch was neutral beige, which perfectly matched our palm tree and monkey drapes. Not only that, but it was also a perfect fit for the small den. God was transforming this house into a home, just as He said in John 14:3 that He goes to prepare a place for us in heaven. It was evident that He was preparing a home for each girl He would call to be a resident at A Place for Us Ministries.

The Caregivers

The home was complete, inside and outside. Every corner was scrubbed, every decorative detail was put into place, and every "*i*" had been dotted and every "*t*" crossed with the fire marshal and with DHEC; yet we were missing a key ingredient: houseparents. These people would implement day-to-day living in a structured environment. Many of the girls that would come into the program would not have a sense of what a normal family looked like. Some would not know how to cook, clean, or manage their time. The house staff would show them how to do these things and more. An important part of the day would be nightly devotions and prayer. The house staff would also manage the cleaning schedule and the grocery menu and arrange transportation to doctor and dentist appointments. Essentially, they were there for the girls and their needs, just like parents would be for their children. As we began to interview applicants, it became evident that Julie and Richard (along with their son, Nicholas) would be our first houseparents. They were a blessing in the lives of each girl that came into the program while at the temporary home. This couple worked hard, and both possessed a servant's heart toward these girls. As with any home, nothing is peaceful or good all the time, but through prayer and a heart's desire to please God, they stayed and ministered to the girls at A Place for Us.

For them, it was a sacrifice to serve in this way because we were walking in faith and did not have much funding to pay full-time house staff since all of our funding was solely through the kindness of individuals, churches, and organizations who knew about us. At this early stage, word had not yet spread about who we were and what we were trying to accomplish; therefore the money to hire them in the first place was strictly by faith. Work was hard, and time off was little. With four pregnant girls living under the same roof, each with her own unique needs, sometimes it seemed impossible to run a peace-filled home. This couple helped us realize that being houseparents required sufficient time off so that they would be refreshed and re-energized to be able to serve the girls more effectively. This was not a job; it was a calling. Looking back, I am sure that their lives were touched and will be forever changed through each girl that entered the doors of the temporary home. Thank you, Julie and Richard, for each life that you touched along with ours.

Peace

This temporary home served some remarkable young people who were different in many ways but who all needed healing from various forms of hurts in their lives. We will never forget the third girl who came through those doors; we gave her the name Peace. Before we ever met with this young lady, we spoke with her over the phone. Based on our guidelines, she was actually too old for our program. Making an exception for her and allowing her to come would have to be a decision for the board to make after each member had prayed about the situation. The board quickly came back with the answer "Yes!" Then several of our staff members went to visit Peace at a Motel 8 in town. While visiting with her, we were overwhelmed by her tears. We had never seen someone cry so many tears that her entire shirt was soaking wet. Peace was from another state up north and had relocated to Greenwood with relatives in hopes of having a better life. Unfortunately, when the environment turned unhealthy due to violence and alcohol in the home, Peace, who was in her second trimester of pregnancy, ended up in a hotel room with literally no place to go and no one she could trust. Her family members were very upset that she had gotten pregnant, and the birthfather did not want to take responsibility. She wasn't poverty-stricken in the sense of material things; she had poverty of the heart with deep wounds that could only be healed by Jesus.

Peace later shared that as soon as she arrived on the lake property, a peace came over her. Peace became her "house name" from then on. Peace was the type of person who felt that she had to make things happen. Day by day, she learned to trust the Lord and wait on His timing. As time grew closer for her to give birth, she thought she would be at the hospital in Greenwood with no family to attend the birth of her son. But God had been working in the hearts of her family members, and Peace had a surprise visit from her mother who was there to support her during the birth and for several days after. Doors began to open for her and her beautiful son to have a place to call home once it was time for them to leave A Place for Us. She had decided to stay in Greenwood, and she was able to get a fully furnished apartment. The landlord made a special exception for her and allowed her to stay in the apartment even though she had a baby living with her. The community surrounded her and lavished her with loving support by stocking her pantry. Although her family was still far away, God began to mend all those broken relationships. Peace later told her story at a fundraising dinner where her father came to hear her. As a result, he decided to support the ministry financially so that others might also find the same hope his daughter had found. Years later, several board members attended her wedding, and I read Isaiah 61, our guiding scripture, as part of her wedding ceremony. Peace and her family now live in her home state and are doing well. Writing this story, we can't help but recall the last time we saw Peace's beautiful son. He was four at the time, well-mannered, with blonde hair and blue eyes, and we could clearly see that he loved his mama.

Dan

Later, we were contacted by the grandfather of a young lady named Marie. This man's pastor had watched him and his wife trying desperately to help Marie because her mother was on drugs, and the family structure had completely broken down. Trying to find a place for her, the pastor called the Department of Social Services, and they gave him the phone number for A Place for Us. Marie entered the program, becoming our fourth resident. The father of her baby, Dan, was in prison for dealing drugs. Shortly after Marie came into the home, everyone at the home began to pray for him every night. After about two months, John Wayne and I made a trip to the prison to visit him. This visit was the beginning of the fulfillment of our vision of reaching out to birthfathers by showing them the unconditional love of Christ.

Over the course of Marie's stay, we learned more about Dan's past through Marie's prayer requests for him. Eventually, we were able to connect with him on a more regular basis, mentoring and encouraging him. Dan was simply a product of his environment. Although he was only nineteen years old, he had been doing drugs for seven years, a result of his parents' addictions. When he was very young, his father had died of a drug overdose. His mother was also on drugs and alcohol, so she had not been able to give him the love and nurturing that he had needed growing up. As a result, he was not comfortable with hugs from members of the ministry; he would not return hugs when people tried to hug him. You see, in order to know how to give love you have to have received love. Dan had never truly experienced this type of love; he thought that there were conditions to be met with every act of kindness. After his release from prison, he continued on a path of destruction. However, one night he came into Greenwood and attended a youth crusade with the ministry. There he accepted Jesus as his personal Lord and Savior. Returning to his hometown went well for a few days until he found himself again in the same old things with the same old people. He began to live from house to house, and his only motivation in life was to find where he would get his next high. Still, every night the residents and the staff continued praying for him.

While his girlfriend was still in our program, things began to suddenly turn for him after his mother overdosed on drugs and died. With both of his parents dying premature deaths due to drugs, Dan came to a crossroad; he would either choose a life filled with drugs, or he would choose another way, God's way. A Place for Us was there to offer him hope by continuing to show him there was a plan for his life, and it was for his good (Jeremiah 29:11). Through our counsel, Dan decided to go to rehab and entered the Faith Home, a program for men struggling with alcohol and drug addiction.

As his story unfolded before us, we were all touched by how God was restoring someone once bound by prison chains and then setting him truly free. This young man would go on to powerfully impact the future of the ministry by sharing his story at "The Father's Love" fundraising banquet. When Dan shared how God had worked in his life, bringing redemption and restoration, many others were also touched, and many hearts were moved to give financial support to A Place for Us. Also, Dan had been praying for a job. That night, one of our supporters who had attended the dinner approached him and offered him a job with benefits.

Dan went on to share his testimony at different events where his story touched many young people's lives. He would come by to visit staff and encourage us in the Lord. He donated books and other encouraging materials that were impacting his life so that we could share them with others. That loving little boy inside had come to life. He loved everyone and always wanted to share with others the love that Jesus had given to him. He no longer resisted hugs, but offered them with ease and joy.

Dan is now living with an uncle and working in his hometown. This chapter is only part of his story; we are certain the Lord is not finished with him yet. When Dan was at Faith Home, he felt the Lord calling him into ministry. We know when God begins a work, He always completes it, and we know that in God's time, this calling will be fulfilled.

Desirae

I have to share just one more story that, still to this day, reminds me of how God's timing is amazing. We received a phone call from a lady from the lower part of the state. She said her daughter, Desirae, was about seven months pregnant and needed a place to stay. The mother's husband, Desirae's stepfather, would not allow her back into the house once he found out that she was pregnant. Listening to this precious mother's heart breaking as she shared her daughter's desperate situation, Lesa Jefferies and I were deeply touched. This mom had paid for two nights in a motel for her daughter, but now, since nothing else had opened up for her, she would be on the streets that night. She wanted Desirae to come into our home, but neither of them drove, and they had no one who could drive her. This meant that Lesa and I would need to drive down there to get her. That very day, we headed out to make the three-hour drive. Once there, we found her in a run-down hotel. She was so sad and lonely—not a trace of a smile on her face. She had not yet been to the doctor because she feared what would happen once everyone knew she was pregnant. An amazing thing happened, though, during this trip—something we will never forget about Desirae. When we went into the hotel room, we could hardly tell that she was pregnant; this young lady who was seven months pregnant was barely showing. After we arrived at the ministry home, it was as if the baby had blossomed, and her belly had grown during the three-hour trip to her new temporary home.

Prior to picking her up, Lesa and I had discussed how God had impressed upon my heart the need to share with her about Jesus—how much He loved her and how she could begin a relationship with Him. It seemed as if there was an urgency about this since her time would be short due to her being in her last trimester. At this point, I had never done this with anyone, believe it or not. This does confirm God's word that says He uses the "foolish things to confound the wise" (I Corinthians 1:27 NKJV). Here I was; I had started a ministry and had never asked anyone if they had received Jesus as their Lord and Savior. However, after we picked her up, we spoke very little; we just sensed that she was tired and did not want to talk. After such a long ride home, we decided not to stay long, so we helped her get settled in for the night and left. However, as we were getting into the car, Lesa asked, "Did you talk to her about what you said God asked you to share with her?"

I replied, "No."

Lesa said, "Then you better get back out and go in and do it. If God told you to do that, you better get back out of this car."

She was right! Hesitantly, I got back out of the car and went in. I was not sure what or how I was supposed to do this, but I knew that I had to be obedient to what God had asked me to do. So I just began to tell Desirae that I was not sure how long she would be with us, but, for some reason, I did not think it would be long. I told her that I really felt the Lord wanted me to share with her how much He loved her. So I asked her if she was a Christian. She timidly replied, "No. I'm not ready for that." I sensed her nervousness.

Realizing that she thought I was going to make her leave, I said, "It's ok. You do not have to be a Christian to come to A Place for Us or to stay at our home, but I do hope you will feel God's love so much in the time that you are here, that before you leave, you will decide that you don't want to leave without Him." I explained to her that she had many decisions to make, and only God Himself could lead her to what would be best for her and her baby. Like most girls who find themselves in this situation, Desirae had to decide if she would parent or make an adoption plan. I told her that if she accepted a relationship with Jesus, then He would talk with her and show her which way she was to go because John 10:27 states that His sheep hear His voice. Knowing that she was tired, and the hour was late, I simply prayed with her and left for the evening. The next day, even after a good night's sleep, she still did not have much to say. The following day, the houseparents gave her a Bible with her name on it, and amazingly, she never laid it down. She carried it around with her and cried all day.

The following week, she had her first appointment with the doctor. There, she received the shocking news that she was due in two weeks! We had thought we had at least eight weeks to work with her, but it now appeared that her stay would be even shorter. She began to talk with an adoption agency to consider her options.

Every day she continued to carry her Bible around with her—still not talking very much and still confused about whether to parent or to place her baby for adoption. Yet even with her silence, I could see that things were taking place within her heart.

The day came all too quickly for her to go to the hospital. As she packed her bags to go, there was one thing that would not be left behind, and that was the Bible that had been given to her. While waiting on the nurses to get everything ready, she asked me to pray with her. I was glad to do that, and as I have done so many times, I said "Let's turn to a page in the Bible to see if God has something He would like to share with you in His Word." We opened the Bible, and it just "happened" to turn to John 10:27, the same passage I had shared with her at the beginning of her stay—about His sheep hearing His voice!

Desirae had the baby by C-section and needed to come back to the home for a few days until she was recovered enough to travel. Although the original plan had been for her to place the baby with adoptive parents, her mother worked it out with her husband for Desirae to go back home and parent the baby. However, she knew that she had some unfinished business to take care of before she could return to her hometown. She told the staff that, if she was able to walk down the church aisle on the following Sunday morning, she was going to go down to the altar and give her life to Jesus.

We may not have known that Desirae would only be with us those few short weeks, but the Lord did. And He was able to accomplish what He wanted in that short period of time. Desirae returned home with her mother. The last time we spoke with her, she was parenting and working on her GED, and things were going well.

Build It, and They Will Come

After all the hard work and prayer, someone who was in a leadership role at another ministry asked me a question. I don't know if this question was asked in order for me to re-think if I was on the right track or if it was meant to cause undue fear to rise within me, but all the same the question was posed. The question was, "What if the house is finished, and the table is set, and no one calls?" The answer that quickly came to me was, "If God does all of this, then He already knows who will come." Sure enough, it wasn't long before we received our first call, and the rest is history. The table continues to be set, and the calls continue to come.

Our faith became sight. As we reflect back over that small, quaint house, many faces, memories, and miracles come to mind, and they *will never be* forgotten. The temporary home was just the beginning of our faith increasing day by day—never to be the same!

Later, the church sold the temporary home. We had purchased land, and now a permanent home would need to be built at the cost of $385,000. Where would we get this kind of money, and how long would it take?

Many more God stories were yet to unfold. They would be nothing we had asked for but more than we had hoped...

A Place in My Heart

Charity's Story

But Mary treasured up all these things and
pondered them in her heart.
Luke 2:19 NIV

Isn't it amazing to think about the challenges Mary, the mother of Jesus, faced? Although she was a virgin, God chose a teenage mother to give birth to His Son. She went through many of the same obstacles faced by many of the girls that come to A Place for Us: her parents' reaction to the news, "I am pregnant and not married" and the town's whispers and stares. Then there was Joseph. Mary may have nervously waited and wondered as her betrothed struggled and grappled with what he should do about her and this baby: "Will he support me and be there for this baby?" "Will he still marry me?" And what about the Christmas journey—knocking on doors, searching for a place to rest, but "there was no room for them in the inn"? (Luke 2:7 NIV) Mary's thoughts were possibly echoing those of our girls: "Where will I have my baby? Must I travel far? Will there be a place for us?" And sometimes our girls must make sacrifices in one way or another. Mary understood that as well, for her Baby eventually became a Sacrifice to save the world and accomplish God's purposes.

Everyone faced with an unplanned pregnancy has many decisions to make. As you read Charity's story, you will see that there is a path planned out for each child and mother. When they allow God's light to shine on each step they take, He will show them the way.

Tammie:

The day Charity came to Lake Greenwood to tour the home is one I will never forget. I could see the shame and guilt all over her face. I was amazed at what a beautiful girl she was, but at this point in her life, there was nothing inside of her that made her feel beautiful. When I told her, "You are a beautiful girl," she barely looked up to smile. She could not believe this was being said to her, a sixteen-year-old pregnant girl.

Charity:

I first heard about A Place for Us Ministries when I was sixteen years old. I was a junior in high school and about five months pregnant. I was told that I would be living at this maternity home some two hours away from my house for the rest of my pregnancy. As you can imagine, that was a scary thing to hear when you are sixteen.

I was in the first group of girls to go through A Place for Us. I remember everything about my first night there. I remember the dinner conversation. I remember the prayer that was prayed over our meal, and I remember thinking about how lonely I was going to feel in such a faraway place with strangers.

But the funny thing is I did not end up feeling lonely during my time at A Place for Us. I felt accepted and loved. Now I'm not sure that this would be an easy task to take on. Think about it; who would welcome a random sixteen-year-old who, by the way, is pregnant, emotionally unstable, and obviously rebellious, to come live with them for a while? There is no denying it; anyone who would be willing to accept God's calling for them to take on the job of loving and living with emotional, unstable pregnant women is truly a brave warrior of Christ. I am sure there were days when all of those who came into contact with me had to pray a little bit harder and bite their tongue a little bit more just to deal with me. But I thank God that these people listened to Him when He called them to begin this ministry.

Tammie:

We would later learn that not only was she beautiful on the outside but on the inside as well. Although Charity will go on to say how we touched her life, she really made a mark on our lives that will never be forgotten. Her stay at A Place for Us really taught the entire staff and board about adoption and how beautiful it can be when God is in it. Many days and nights, both Charity and the staff shed tears. But, as God began to work out the details, there was no way you could doubt she was doing the right thing because God was all about the details.

Charity:

As I continued my journey through my pregnancy at A Place for Us, I started to look into placing my baby for adoption. I visited several adoption agencies, spoke with many different adoption advocates, and looked at many, many family profiles. I finally found the family that God had set aside for my child. This family had struggled with infertility for many years and had already been through the adoption experience with their other two children. The father had been a youth pastor for many years; so they could relate to kids my age.

I decided that if I was going to place my child up for adoption, I wanted to have an open relationship with her adoptive family. I wanted to be able to share in the life of my child but also be able to provide her with a stable home from the start. An open adoption was the only option for me as far as I was concerned, and the family I chose for my child was in total agreement with the decision. They too wanted my child to know who I was and that I placed her with them out of love and concern for her future.

I had really prayed for a family that was in or near the state of South Carolina so I could see my child several times a year and be present in her life from the start. But God had a different plan; this family, though they seemed nearly perfect, lived half-way across the country. The hardest part of deciding on this family was the fact that I was pretty certain that, with the distance between us, I would have very little physical contact with my child.

When I called the adoptive parents to let them know that I had chosen them to parent my child, they agreed to come and meet me in person before I delivered. They flew down to meet me, and I knew from that point on that God really did know what He was doing. I had shared with them both over the phone in one of our first conversations that I had chosen a name for my child. They were curious as to what that name was. I told them, "Sophie," and they really didn't say too much at the time. When they came to meet me in person, we talked about everyday stuff, and they kind of worked up to actually talking about the adoption and what my expectations were, as well as theirs. It was kind of an awkward conversation to have at first. It is very difficult to talk about giving your baby to someone. However, somewhere in that conversation, the mother let me know that they had talked about it and felt that Sophie would be the perfect name for our baby.

Tammie:

Charity had become friends with another girl in the program who was only fourteen years old, and she had decided to parent. These two girls bonded, and they loved each other like sisters. They both chose to respect each other for the decisions they were individually making about their babies. Both decisions—to parent or to bless another couple with your baby—were difficult paths.

For Charity, what she would soon go through finally began to hit home. Many nights the house staff would hear Charity banging her head against the shower, her heart tearing in two as she wailed and cried. (If any person reading this book ever believed that your birth-mother did not love you because she placed you for adoption, our prayer is that, after reading this story, you will see that this is the greatest sacrificial love ever given. I am sure you were loved to the "moon and back" to have a mother who chose life for you.) Never has there been a mother who educated herself more on parenting and adoption (and even on child-birthing) than Charity.

Charity:

Several weeks after that first meeting, Sophie was born. I spent three days in the hospital with her. And then it was time for us to go home. Sophie's adoptive parents and their other two children came to the hospital to meet Sophie and to take her home. Of all the good and bad days I have experienced in my life since that day, I can still remember that day almost in its entirety. I can remember the attorneys coming in with all the paperwork. I can remember Sophie's adoptive parents and their children and all the words being spoken in that room as I tried to keep a brave face. I can remember reaching a point at which I thought I was going to scream from holding in all my emotions - at which point, I took Sophie into the bathroom and locked myself in and just sobbed. I can remember the nurse that wheeled me and Sophie out to the parking lot. I even remember the nurse hugging me and asking me if I was going to be okay. I remember whispering over and over and over again into Sophie's little ear, "I will always be your mommy, I love you." I remember handing my little baby to a woman I had met only once before. I remember the ride home with my mom. I remember collapsing in exhaustion when we finally got back to my parents' home. I remember the days and weeks that followed that day and how alone and empty I felt.

There were a lot of difficult memories from that day. There were a lot of moments that I relived in my head many times over for the next several years. There were sounds and smells and sights that reminded me of the heartache I had experienced. There was a point where I could not even see babies or young mothers without experiencing an emotional breakdown.

But there was something in the midst of all that darkness and pain, something that somehow made it bearable. There was a steady, constant love that flowed out from my family and the family I had made through A Place for Us. The same people that greeted me at the door the first day I arrived at A Place for Us have been there for me every day since.

These people have never forgotten about me or stopped checking in on me or stopped loving me. I didn't walk out of that hospital and walk out of the lives of those who are involved with A Place for Us. They saw my tears and they prayed even harder. They encouraged me a little more. They reached out further. They showed me that I could turn a tough, seemingly devastating situation into a positive platform for young people my age.

Tammie:

When God is the Author of adoption it has to be a beautiful thing. Throughout the Bible, there are stories of people who had been adopted who saved a nation: Esther and Moses and—not to mention—Jesus. Jesus was adopted and then, in turn, adopts us to Himself. While Charity lived in the home, many nights we would share countless stories about the God things that had happened to start the ministry of A Place for Us. Charity would sit and listen intently, and one night she spoke up and said, "I want my own stories just like the ones you are sharing about A Place for Us."

Charity:

I began to share my story with other girls that came through A Place for Us. Then I shared my story with groups of students at several schools. I was able to use my experience as a platform for educating and relating to my peers.

A lot has happened in my life since the day I handed Sophie to her new family. I finished the school year and went on to complete my senior year of high school on time. I have since graduated from college with a degree in nursing and am proud to call myself a Registered Nurse. I am now enrolled in a Master's degree program. Sophie is now seven years old. She is in school and is thriving. She is smart, outgoing, and beautiful (if I do say so myself).

Tammie:

Well, as you might expect, Charity too had many answered prayers and her own God stories to share with others. God restored her relationship with her father, who had been crushed and disappointed by her actions. Charity expressed that her father wasn't one to cry easily; however, when this sweet baby girl was born, he too cried many tears. Charity also realized that God wasn't the big God Who was way up in heaven, but He was right there with her.

Charity's story came full circle on a very sunny, warm day in July of 2009. Beautiful Sophie, one of Charity's greatest treasures in human form, walked down the aisle of a church as Charity's flower girl at her wedding. What a beautiful gift from God! Watching the precious interactions between this birthmother and the daughter she had placed in the arms of loving parents, we stood in awe of such a beautiful friendship.

Charity:

I had the wonderful honor of having Sophie to be the flower girl in my wedding in July of 2009. At the rehearsal dinner the night before our wedding, Sophie came to me like we were old friends. She talked with me about her friends, her gymnastic abilities, and about how much we were alike even though we had not seen each other in over three years. She knew and identified me as her birth mom and was quite proud of that. She had not even seen me since she was barely three years old, and yet she stayed with me that evening as if we were longtime playmates.

Now I don't know everything there is to know about God and how He works in life. But, I'm pretty sure that He realized how stressed out I was going to be on my wedding day, and He was gracious enough to bless my time with Sophie by allowing her to remember or relate to the unspoken bond that we share as mother and daughter. There were no forced moments; there was no coercion between my bridal party and Sophie as the flower girl. There were only good memories that will forever have a place in my heart.

A Place for Us is not just a maternity home that helps pregnant women get through a tough time in life. This home is a safe place for the souls of these women to rest and regroup and re-evaluate their beliefs, dreams and goals in life.

Have you ever experienced true love from a complete stranger for absolutely no good reason? I mean honest-to-goodness unconditional true love for doing nothing? I have. I have experienced love from complete and total strangers for no reason except this: they were showing me the same love and acceptance they had experienced from Christ Jesus for doing absolutely nothing as well.

A Place for Us is a home where girls of all ages and backgrounds take refuge during their time of need and crisis. While living at A Place for Us, these girls continue their education and receive practical lessons in cooking and keeping up a household. They go through child-birthing classes (if pregnant) and both parenting and adoption workbooks. These girls also go to weekly Bible studies and attend church service each Sunday. However, the most important thing these girls experience is daily, up-close examples of Christ's love for them. In the face of each house staff, each board member, and each volunteer, these girls see Christ.

The people at A Place for Us not only invest in just a short period of time with these girls but they are in it for the long haul. They are there for these girls long after they leave the home. Tammie and her husband, Bonnie and her husband, Lesa and many others were there the night I walked into the world of A Place for Us. They prayed for me as I struggled with making difficult decisions about my life and my child's life. They supported me as I looked for an adoptive family for my child, and they rejoiced with me when God showed me who that family should be. They greeted my daughter the day she was born and cried with me the day that I handed her to her new mother. They were there the day I graduated from high school and prayed me on through college. And they were there by my side six years after the day I met them to pray over my coming marriage and to read scripture in my wedding.

As that scared pregnant sixteen-year-old little girl, I was not alone. And as a twenty-three-year-old college graduate I was not forgotten. I was loved by complete and total strangers for nothing I had done. I was loved beyond my pregnancy, beyond my teenage years, beyond all reasoning and understanding; these people still loved me. They made a commitment to God to do His work for His people through this ministry, and they kept their word.

The end and yet the beginning.

Tammie:

Charity felt our love, and in turn she poured out her love on us in such a powerful and compelling way. About three years after Charity left the program of A Place for Us, she returned to attend the visitation for our son who was tragically killed in an automobile accident. Her wise words brought to us all much love and comfort. She said, "You were there to hold me when I let my baby go; now I am here for you when you must let your son go." What the ministry had poured out upon her, she was now able to give back to us in such a powerful way.

Charity and her husband recently were blessed with twin baby girls. This is such a great witness of God's restoration and redemptive love for Charity. She now has a wonderful and loving husband, a son, and twin daughters. We are sure that she and her family will continue to have many more God stories to share throughout their lifetimes.

My name is Charity...and my story matters.

Never Alone

Karen's Story

I'll stay with you, I'll protect you wherever you go,
and I'll bring you back to this very ground.
I'll stick with you until I've done
everything I promised you.
Genesis 28:15 The Message Bible

To a young girl growing into womanhood, life happens quickly, but not quickly enough. That only seems a cliché for one living in this ever-changing time of life, but this is where my story begins. I was eighteen years old and in love. And even though high school had always been important to me, it seemed at this time in my life, finishing school was not important on my agenda for life. So before even graduating from high school, I left home and got married. I believed that life was finally happening for me. My knight in shining armor came and swept me off my feet. I was finally seeing my dreams come true, and my life could not be any better. I soon became pregnant and had a beautiful baby daughter. I loved and cared for my daughter and husband as most wives and mothers do, but much to my dismay, my life began to change. I was seeing my husband change; his personality and his emotions were changing; he was becoming more and more unpredictable and abusive. I soon found out that he was using drugs. I knew that I could not and would not live like this or allow our daughter to be raised in this type of environment, so I left. This separation did not last long; I had a dependence on my husband that I could not explain. I thought each time I went back that he would change, but he didn't. He and I were separated nine times before I had finally had enough. During all the turmoil, I lost my sense of reality; I lost myself to the fear and the lack of control, and I started using drugs. I knew that I could not raise my daughter with this addiction and gave my mother temporary custody of her.

What began as a thought in my mind simmered and became an ever-constant need in my waking hours. My addiction began to overtake me and take control of my life. It was a disease of my spirit, and I allowed this need, this dependence, to control me and lead me down a road where I felt I could not step off. By this time, my divorce was final, and I was living with a boyfriend in conditions that were not suitable for anyone; but all these consequences were due to the unhealthy, selfish choices I had been making. I was drinking alcohol, smoking marijuana, taking pills, and making and smoking methamphetamine. It was during this time that I found out that I was pregnant again. I was in a situation that I did not want to be in. I had every intention of getting an abortion, but my mother intervened. She asked me to come home. I knew that I would be safe there and would be able to have my daughter once again in my life, but I knew I could not stay there. I had been out on my own and did not see where I would be able to give over control of my life in order to live there and abide by my mom's rules. By this time I was a spiritual, emotional, and physical wreck, and I was going through withdrawal. It was then that my choices landed me in the psychiatric unit of the local hospital.

I spent both Christmas and New Years in this ward of the hospital. My head and body were beginning to clear, and I was seeing some light in my circumstances, but the darkness in my life was bigger than the glimpses of light I could see. When it was time for me to be released from the hospital, my mother was not willing to allow me to come back home because of my prior behavior. The hospital staff had been looking for alternative opportunities for me. During their search, they found an opening in a maternity home, but it was too far away for my liking. I refused to be placed there because I felt the distance was too great for Mom to bring my daughter, who was now four years old, to visit. The only other option I was offered was a bus ticket to take me to a homeless shelter. I knew that this could not and would not be the option that I would choose. I became angry—with both the hospital and my mom because I felt like neither one of the presented choices was good enough for me.

In desperation, I began leafing through the phone book, calling every place that I could find that I thought would be able to help me. I called a local children's home, and they referred me to A Place for Us Ministries. Tammie Price, the director of the home came to the hospital to visit me. She explained how the program worked, gave me an application, and prayed with me.

I was still not sure what I wanted to do, but because I was determined not to go to the homeless shelter or to a maternity home that was far away, I decided to go to A Place for Us. I made up my mind to prove my mother and the hospital wrong. I did not need to go far away to get help; I could find the help that I needed right here in my own community.

Once I arrived at the ministry home, I became involved in the program and stayed very busy. I participated in several classes and

Bible studies and did chores in the home, but my life was compli-cated. I was still feeling the need to see my mental health coun-selor on a regular basis. I would become agitated and angry that I could not be taken as frequently as I wanted to be. Tammie finally confronted me in her usual kind and caring disposition and let me know that there were times and seasons for counseling and that I did not need to let someone else make this important decision for me. She told me that I needed to sit back, read God's Word, and listen for the answer that the Great Counselor, Jesus Christ, would tell me. She reminded me that He would speak to me; all I had to do was ask Him for the things I needed and then listen. I knew Tammie was right. I knew that I did need to address the issues and questions that had accumulated in my life so that I would be able to make the best decision about whether to parent my baby or make an adoption plan; but decision-making was hard for me at this time.

I was keeping in contact with Mom. Because of my past his-tory, she felt very strongly that I should make an adoption plan for the baby, and after listening to her thoughts about this situation, I made the decision for adoption.

Although it was a difficult decision, I knew it was the right one. I wanted my baby to have both a mother and a father. This was so important to me because my father had never been around much, and my daughter's father was never around either. I also wanted my baby to have a family with strong Christian values. After several visits with my mother and a Mennonite family who were friends of my mother, I began to think that I might want to place my baby with a Mennonite family. I was able to spend some time with this family and learn about their culture. I knew that my baby deserved a good family, and I was so thankful that my mother was there to help me make a wise decision. She suggested that I research the possibility of placing my baby with a Mennonite family. At first, it was a difficult task, but I did not give up or stop praying; neither did Mom or anyone else. I knew that God would answer our prayers. It was during this time that I began to actually experience and know the healing that was taking place in Mom's and my relationship. We were becoming closer than we had ever been. I was seeing first-hand how God paints a masterpiece in His time.

I am not good at waiting. Through my situation and circumstances, I was being taught the blessings of waiting on and for God's hand to work, one second at a time, one hour at a time, and one day at a time. Finally, I found the perfect family. Mom and I were able to meet this family and spend some time with them. We even had a baby shower for my baby's adoptive mother, and I presented her with a baby blanket that I had crocheted. We corresponded with letters until the delivery time grew close. It was then that they came and stayed close by.

In my heart, I knew the adoption was going to be very difficult for me. So I had decided on a closed adoption; I didn't want to even see my baby when she was born. I was convincing myself that it would be easier for me that way. The staff at A Place for Us continued to encourage me to keep praying and assured me that they would continue to pray for me, my baby, and the family that would be blessed by this gift I was about to deliver.

Finally, the big day came and I went into labor. I had the housemother and my labor coach with me. Mom even came to the hospital when she was given the news that I was in labor. This labor was difficult for me, and my baby was born with a hole in one of her lungs. She had to be rushed straight to the NICU upon her birth. At this point, I changed my mind about seeing my baby. I just had to see her. I needed to hold her. My daughter spent a week in the NICU, and everyone from Mom to the adoptive family and some close friends came to visit me and the baby as much as possible.

Then the day came when the baby was ready to be released. This meant the time had come for me to sign the adoption papers. My mother, having bonded with her precious granddaughter, did not think she could live with the decision of letting her go live forever with another family; but I told her she had to do it, it was the right thing, and it was for the best; this was the decision that I had made.

We went to spend some time with the baby before the attorney came with the adoption papers. As I sat in the rocking chair, cradling my daughter in my arms, for a moment I began to doubt the decision I had made. My mother called the houseparents at A Place for Us to come and talk with us downstairs in the hospital. There we talked and prayed. The houseparents told me that there was no right or wrong choice; I just needed to follow my heart. In those wise words I found freedom and knew that I needed to follow through with the decision I had made that would provide the best future for my daughter. I then had the courage to go back to the NICU and sign the adoption papers. I was able to hold my daughter a little while after signing the papers. Mom came over to us and gently took my baby and placed her in the arms of her new mother. That was one of the hardest days of my life.

A few days after the birth of my baby, there was a dedication service for her at a local Mennonite church. There were many people in attendance that had been a part of my life and would be a part of my daughter's future. It was a beautiful event, and the memories are etched in my mind and will remain with me forever.

The many miracles that God blessed me with did not stop here, however. He spoke to me with a peace that caused me to rethink my decision about the closed adoption. I changed my mind to make my daughter's adoption an open adoption, which has been a wonderful blessing. With this decision, I can call, write, and even visit my daughter if I want to. I even made a scrapbook for her so she can know about her birth family. Her adoptive parents will be able to share the scrapbook with her when they feel the timing is right.

After leaving A Place for Us, I was able to return home to my mother's house to live. God has definitely done a miraculous work in many of my relationships since my time spent at A Place for Us. I have learned to rely on the Wonderful Counselor to meet my every need. In time, I was able to regain custody of my oldest daughter, and since that time have gone on to earn three college degrees and multiple certificates.

Being at A Place for Us was a true blessing to me. My word to all who read my story is, "I learned what true love, faith, hope, and prayer are all about. I discovered things about myself that I had never known before, and I learned that I am NEVER all alone." Currently as this book is being written, I am back in college working on my bachelors to masters program. Thank you, God, for making a way for me.

My name is Karen...and my story matters.

Be Still

The Red Sea Story

Truly I tell you, whatever you did for one of the least of these brothers and sisters of mine, you did for Me.
Matthew 25:40

This is what I want you to do: Ask the Father for whatever is in keeping with the things I've revealed to you. Ask in My name, according to My will, and He'll most certainly give it to you. Your joy will be a river overflowing its banks!
John 16:24 The Message Bible

There is a story in the Bible that talks about God parting the waters of the Red Sea. The people of Israel had left their slavery in Egypt and were traveling to the land God had promised them. The Egyptian soldiers were chasing them to bring them back into slavery. They ended up stuck between the Red Sea and the Egyptians. God had Moses stretch out his hand over the sea, and all that night the Lord drove the sea back with a strong east wind, parting the waters so that there was a wall of water on the right and a wall of water on the left. God's people walked across on dry ground. It wasn't mushy mud or wet sand; it was dry ground (Exodus 14:19-22). If God could part the waters of the Red Sea so that His people walked across on dry ground, do you suppose He could work to re-route water to bring it to our dry land?

We had already purchased the land, and our "fish story" friend Larry had graciously graded it free of charge. Our next step before we could begin building our permanent home was to dig a well. We figured the minimum cost of digging a well would be around $4,000. We knew a few people in the community who dug wells, so we assumed that God would send one of them to dig a well for us as He had done with the grading, but we soon learned that it was not going to be that simple.

Because this home would be a group home for girls, there were state regulations, which had to be followed. As with the temporary home, there must be a fire hydrant within five hundred feet of the house. We began researching how we could do this since we were in the county, and public water was not available. We noticed there was a fire hydrant about half a mile from the home. So we called the Commission of Public Works (CPW) to see what we could do to have them bring water down the road just half a mile. We discovered that CPW was not authorized to run a waterline any further than where it was. There had been a two-year lawsuit over this issue, and those were the parameters set by the court. Therefore, any waterline on our property would have to be run by Donalds-Due West Water (DDWW) because they had the right of way.

I contacted DDWW to see if they would consider running the waterline. Much to my surprise, the person who answered the phone happened to be a friend of the ministry and a former hair client. After I told him our situation, he said that he understood but didn't give me any hope that this issue could be resolved and a waterline established. He said that he would have to go to the board of directors to find out how they could help us, but he already knew that they would not have the money to run the waterline. The only way they could afford to put in a waterline would be if they could get a grant. He also doubted they would be willing to allow CPW to run a line to the home. At this point, it seemed highly unlikely that we would be able to get a waterline to our land.

The wait seemed endless, but two weeks later, we finally got the call from DDWW. They had decided to grant CPW the right of way for this situation only. CPW could run the waterline only to our land and no further. Ecstatic, we called CPW to tell them the good news; however, their response deflated our excitement. We felt as if we were on a roller coaster—shot to the top with the first call, and then suddenly crashing back down to the bottom with the second call. CPW stated that they did not see a way they could afford the $47,000 it would take to run this line. Searching quickly for a way to resolve this, I suddenly asked, "If we paid your employees would you allow them to run the line?" Their answer was a firm "No" because they believed that we would more than likely call with repeated complaints because we would be at the end of the waterline, and the water would not run clear. Having to come flush it out frequently would be an added expense that they were not willing to cover.

Baffled at this point, I could not understand why God had provided the money we needed to purchase this land if we were not going to be able to get water to it. One day, my daughter-in-law Valerie called me. She could tell that I was extremely upset; I explained that I had just gotten off the phone with CPW and had received very disappointing news. I just didn't see a way that we were going to be able to build the home without that waterline. She told me, "You don't need to worry about it. That land is God's land, and if He wants water there, it is going to happen." She went on to say, "If God parted the Red Sea, then surely He can bring water to His own property!" I sat there stunned by her words; then joy filled my heart at this reminder of God's miraculous power to accomplish impossible things like putting in a waterline!

Day after day, as we made calls, the thought consuming my mind was, "How can we get a fire hydrant within five hundred feet of the home in order to meet the fire codes?" I thought that maybe we could by-pass the need for a waterline and just dig a well. One day I called the local fire marshal because we had heard there was a possibility that we could have what they call a dry fire hydrant if the house was near a creek. During this particular call, he agreed to send someone out to test the water in our creek to determine if it was deep enough. However, while I was waiting for him to schedule a time, he accidentally hung up. My immediate thought was, "I can't believe the fire marshal just hung up on me!" However, within a couple of minutes, he called back and said, "I'm sorry I hung up on you. I wanted to call back and tell you one more thing." He said, "Mrs. Price, do you know that God parted the Red Sea, and the Israelites walked through on dry ground?" With those words, my heart stood still. I could not believe my ears! The local fire marshal was confirming what had already been spoken over this situation!

I asked him, "Who told you that is what God has been saying?"

He responded, "No one told me anything. I just wanted to tell you what God has been showing me and my wife for our situation." Then he shared his personal story of standing in faith against impossible odds. This confirmation was only one of many. For weeks, it seemed that every message, every book, every song that came our way was about the Red Sea, and soon we began to realize that "with God, all things are possible" (Matthew 19:26 NIV). Somehow, God would bring water and a fire hydrant to this property. I just had to keep reminding myself that this property was His, and it would be for His glory, and it would be for His children. "And all who see them will acknowledge that they are a people that the Lord has blessed" (Isaiah 61:9b NIV).

"Be still and know that I am God" (Psalm 46:10 KJV) was also a resounding message inside my heart. As we traveled past the land day after day, we continued to wait on God. It's funny how we have always heard, "God is always on time, but sometimes it feels like He is never a minute early." We were still waiting on an answer. In many ways, we were similar to the Israelites who kept experiencing God's faithfulness yet kept wondering if He was going to come through.

But God kept sending us messages throughout this entire ordeal, reminding us that He parted the Red Sea, and nothing was too hard for Him (Genesis 18:14).

This situation was becoming one of our biggest obstacles, yet it would turn out to be one of our greatest lessons. As our faith was being challenged to the core, we were being stretched by circumstances that were the opposite of what we knew God was saying. Some days, we were tempted to give in to the doubt and discouragement. CPW tested the creek and found that it was not deep enough for us to have a dry fire hydrant. We were back to square one because CPW still was not budging from their refusal to put in a waterline even if WE provided the money to pay their workers. How were we going to get water and have the required fire hydrant? The construction of the house was on hold because the grant that we needed would not be approved without proof that we had water on the property. Not giving up, but feeling the doubt trying to creep in, I called CPW yet again. The Holy Spirit must have directed this conversation because my question probably shocked me as much as it shocked the man on the other end of the phone. I asked, "If the Lord puts it on someone's heart to put the waterline in free of charge, would you allow us to buy water from you?" He must have thought, "Well, how can I say 'No' to that?"

He replied, "Well, if God does that, I guess we would let you buy water."

Another miracle was beginning to take shape as other people in the community heard about our water situation and joined their faith with ours. People would give me names of individuals who might be willing to help us. They never said what some of these people did for a living—just that they may be willing to help. So out of obedience (and desperation) I began to make the calls.

My first call was to Charles Sperry of Sperry Services. I was told that he put in waterlines and may give the ministry a discounted price. As usual, I presented the need, asking him to pray about whether the Lord wanted him to help us. Mr. Sperry had never heard of A Place for Us Ministries but listened very intently as I explained our heart and mission and our current need. He said, "Mrs. Price, would you give me a couple of days to pray about this?

I will call you back and let you know what the Lord shows me." Within two days, Mr. Sperry called back and said, "You know what the Lord showed me? He just needs for His people to do His work. I will put the waterline in free of charge. However, I will not be able to supply the materials for the job. That will cost you about $15,000 for supplies, but I know God will provide for it. When you get the resources lined up, let me know, and my crew will put the waterline in at no cost." Although I should not have been surprised, I was awe-struck by God and His power to make the impossible possible!

Still we had obstacles; the ministry did not have $15,000 for the supplies. Then one day at the beauty shop, one of my customers listened to this story and suggested that I contact Joe Chandler who was a good friend of hers. She gave me his number, and I placed it on my office desk along with the other names people had given me to contact. I left it there and didn't call that day because I felt so awkward calling people about our needs, especially when the person was a complete stranger. I did not know what type of business he owned and really was not in the mood to tell the story all over again. While I was battling in my head whether or not I really wanted to pick up the phone and call him, the phone rang. Lillian, one of our supporters and prayer partners, called to say that we might want to call Joe Chandler. It was obvious that God was saying, "Get over yourself and call Joe Chandler!"

In obedience, I called Joe Chandler. This conversation took a little longer than the previous call. Mr. Chandler also wanted to know about the ministry because he too had never heard of it. He seemed to have a lot of people who would contact him quite often asking for help because they knew he had a very giving heart and helped several organizations. He said, "It seems everyone in Greenwood has a need and is asking for something." I let him know I was not asking for anything; I was just trying to be obedient in making the call. He proceeded to tell me what type of business he owned. He put in waterlines. At this point, I told him that Mr. Sperry was putting in the lines; we just needed to provide the materials. He asked how much, and I gave him the footage. He asked me if I realized how much that was going to cost.

By this time, I was prepared for the "No" that I thought I was about to hear. However, surprisingly, he continued to ask questions, and I tried to answer each one to the best of my abilities, but in closing, I simply asked, "Mr. Chandler, would you please pray about why I was given your name to call? And if there is anything you feel you are supposed to do, then you can call me back."

He responded, "Mrs. Price I don't need to call you back, and you won't need to call me back." (I held my breath.) "I already know that I am supposed to donate the waterline. All I need to know now is—where can I deliver it?" He donated everything on our supply list except the fire hydrant.

You see why we call this the Red Sea Story? God held back every hindrance, and He moved the water to our land. Two days later Charles Sperry called back and said that someone had donated a fire hydrant for this job. As the story continued to unfold, the engineer at CPW contacted us and volunteered to use his spare time to do the engineer drawing for us free of charge. CPW agreed to allow the water to be run, and they also waived the hook-up fee. In other words, the waterline did not cost the ministry one penny. What an amazing story! I hope that the next time you face an obstacle in your life, God will remind you that He parted the Red Sea, and the Israelites walked through on dry ground. I want to thank the people in this story that chose to be a Moses and stretched out your hands and your hearts to make it a testimony of God's faithfulness.

As this chapter comes to an end, it is only fitting to remember the quote from Mr. Sperry, "God said He just needs His people to do His work." Just last February, Mr. Sperry went to be with the Lord, and I am sure he heard the words, "Well done, my good and faithful servant." It took two weeks for them to dig out the ditches for the waterlines. Mr. Sperry and his men worked long hours digging through rocks. They tore up their equipment several times, fixed them, and then kept on working. This job that they did for us free of charge was the only work they had during those two weeks. How many cups of water do you suppose these men gave to the least of these? Jesus said in Matthew 10:42, "And if anyone gives even a cup of cold water to one of these little ones who is My disciple, truly I tell you, that person will certainly not lose their reward" (NIV).

These are just a few of the men who gave to see God's work fulfilled. There is no way we can remember every name and every detail involved in the completing of this home, but the beautiful thing is that the Lord remembers them all. We pray God's blessings be continually poured out over every business and every family that gave to the building of this home.

No Crumbs but the Whole Loaf

The Alcoves Story

He brought me out into a spacious place;
He rescued me because He delighted in me.
Psalm 18:19 NIV

I t was the fall of 2005, a time of transition for A Place for Us. The temporary home had been sold, and we were breaking ground to start construction of the permanent home. The board decided not to take any more girls as residents because getting another home up to code would be a time-consuming and expensive process. We would mentor girls that God brought our way but would not house them until the permanent home was finished. Donations of clothes and household products continued to pour in, so the board agreed to begin looking for a location to open an upscale resale clothing boutique that we hoped would serve two purposes. It would give our residents hands-on job training, and it would serve as another means of support for the ministry. We felt this was the perfect timing. A vision that had been on our hearts for at least a year now was about to explode into something greater than any of us had hoped or imagined.

The board said to look, and we certainly looked; sometimes it seemed that we looked so hard that we had a crick in our necks. Every empty building we passed, we would get the number and then call to get a price. At first, the board had agreed to pay $400 a month, but finding a building with rent that low was going to be impossible; so the board increased it to $600 per month. As with every other story, we did not have any extra resources for this new expense. This would have to be done on faith. Looking back, it's hard to believe we even called about the old T.E Jones Furniture Store. Of course, the realtor immediately said, "I don't think you would want this building because it is several thousand dollars a month."

After weeks of calling and looking, a pastor contacted us about a building he had a contract on but had decided not to take. His church was willing to hold the contract until we were able to look at it. It seemed like the perfect place because it was $600 a month, in a good location, and was 3,000 square feet, which we thought was a lot of space. We had tried to rent several other buildings in our price range, but every door was shut. Some explained that they were not interested in renting out space to a second-hand store. After looking at this particular building, every board member agreed to move forward. We contacted the property management, and they confirmed that the church held the contract and that they would honor that contract for us as well. We could bring them a check the next day. Well, we did not have a peace about waiting another day, so we took a check within the hour of that conversation. It was then that we were informed that there was a cross in communication with another realtor, and the property already had a contract on it. They could not take our check to hold the building. First, I was completely shocked. Then I got upset—mostly at the devil, who was trying to stop the plans for the resale store from going forward.

By this time, it was time to head to church, but I was still upset about not getting the building. I ultimately had to put it in God's hands. That evening a member of the church was leading the service. He did not know anything about us looking for a building, but his message is one that I will never forget. He was talking about trusting God when it seems like things are not working out. He went on to say, "As a matter of fact, there is someone here tonight who has been looking for some kind of a building or store, and you think that the devil has taken it away from you. Well, let me tell you something. God has that building waiting for you. But the only thing is that you are willing to settle for the crumbs, but the Lord said He doesn't want you to have the crumbs; He wants you to have the whole loaf of bread!" Wow! That is exactly what the Lord wanted me to hear. The next morning, although I had not seen the loaf of bread and did not know where it was, I knew that message had been for the ministry and that God did not want us to have that building. I knew that whatever He had for us was going to be so much better than the one I thought the devil was trying to steal. God was not allowing the thief to steal anything; instead, He was protecting and providing the best for His children and for His store! "Every good and perfect gift is from above" (James 1:17 NIV).

It took a few more board meetings, a few more phone calls, a few more divine appointments, but through a series of events, God soon pulled together what He had been planning all along. Several months before we got started on this new venture, a lady interested in starting her own ministry called us. She wanted to know how we funded the ministry, so we told her about our future plans to open a resale store. She then suggested that we think "big"; she thought we should not have just a resale store. Instead, we should have extra space to lease out to vendors. It could be like a mini-mall. I told her that we would not be interested in doing that and never gave her comment another thought—at least, not until the Lord brought it back to mind. Shortly after this call, I went to visit my sister in Hendersonville. I was sharing about our desire to locate a building when my brother-in-law out of the blue said, "It's too bad that old furniture store building (T.E. Jones Building) isn't available."

I commented, "Oh, it is, but it costs several thousand dollars a month, and there is no way we would consider paying that much for rent."

Several board meetings down the road, the T.E. Jones building was brought up again. Suzanne thought that we should at least re-visit the idea of renting it. I reminded everyone that we had already checked into this building, and there was no way that we could afford it since it was nearly three times the amount approved. But then I said, "Well, since this has been brought up again, I will share with you all two things that have happened this week." I told them about the phone conversation with the lady and about my brother-in-law's comment. At this point, different members were beginning to see the possibilities. Someone else suggested that we could rent out part of the building to another ministry. We agreed to all go home and pray about it. My plan was to contact another ministry which was looking for a new location for their re-sale store to see if they would be interested in renting out the lower level and the warehouse, also belonging to T.E. Jones. This would at least make it seem more feasible.

That night, one of our board members could not sleep for thinking about this "mini-mall" idea. Elisse Sorrow owned a clothing boutique. Ideas flooded her mind—thoughts inspired by God to show her how it could actually work. She would be more than ready to share at our next board meeting. In the meantime, I contacted the other ministry, but they didn't feel renting our space was the right move for them. Soon the board met to discuss Elisse's ideas. We were getting very excited about where the Lord seemed to be leading us; however, as we began to take steps in that direction, we felt we were up against what appeared to be impossible odds. First, the cost was obviously above our price range. Then another obstacle arose. When we went to the leasing company that was managing the property, we were informed that the owner didn't want to lease to a non-profit again because of a bad experience he had had with another of his rental properties.

Now that we look back at the whole picture we can certainly understand. Our financial statements would have proved there was no way we could pay this large amount of rent. But we knew that our God owned the "cattle on a thousand hills" (Psalm 50:10 NIV), and He can afford anything His heart desires. Well, it was not quite that easy to convince the owner that God would pay our bills every month. However, we have found it to be true that He pays all His bills on time.

Donna Brounkowski suggested that we call Merri Neal, a friend from church who owned a small percentage of the building. Perhaps she could let Mr. Jones know that we were a creditable non-profit ministry. Well, God's Word says that He will go ahead of you, (Isaiah 45:2) and how true that is! When we called Merri Neal, she said that they did own a small percentage of the building but that Mr. Jones was the one who made those decisions. They asked about our plans for the building, and as I began to tell them, they were amazed. The Lord had awakened them the previous night with thoughts of what could be done with that building. They couldn't go back to sleep talking about the T.E. Jones building as ideas began to pop into their minds about a mini-mall set up. As they discussed it, they came to the conclusion that it would be a great idea, but only if you could get the right people in there. Our phone call to them confirmed what God was telling them and showing us. Scott, Merri Neal's husband, later told us that He could not say that there had been a lot of big God things happen to him over the years, but this was one that he would never forget, and neither will we.

Well, when God said he would give us a loaf of bread instead of crumbs, He meant it. Within days, we signed the contract on the old T.E. Jones building which was 22,000 square feet and included a 10,000 square-foot warehouse. The rent was about four times the amount we could afford (or so we thought), but God's accounting is different from ours.

Looking at this empty shell of a building, which had 11,000 square feet on the first floor, we visualized the layout of the store. The first floor would house the mini-mall with the resale store nestled in the back. We decided we needed walls that would make up the small alcove spaces. At this point, everyone we knew was already committed to building the home for the girls, and since we certainly did not want to stop construction to work on the store, our help and resources were very limited. Most people thought we were crazy to try to open a store and build a house at the same time.

It was our hearts' cry that the Lord would make it evident that this is what He wanted us to do and to make it clear that this was His store and His idea. On Thursday, I was cutting hair at the beauty shop. As I worked, I whispered, "Lord, if this is your store, would you please have someone call me about building these walls?" By now, it should come as no surprise that when I got home that evening, the phone had a message blinking on it. It was Dan Fehr, a master craftsman. When I called him back, he said, "I understand from Karen (a recent resident) that you would like to open a store and need some walls built."

I said, "Yes, we were trying to set it up like a mini-mall, but I've already contacted a contractor who said we would need to hire an architect to draw it all out to scale." I let him know that we did not have the resources or the time to do those things because we had set a deadline for opening the store by Black Friday, only a few weeks away. Doubtful that he could help us in such a short amount of time, I was actually a little reluctant to meet with Mr. Fehr, but at the same time, I felt that this could very well be one of those God things. We met the next day; he came in with a piece of paper and a pencil and, within thirty minutes, had drawn out every alcove perfectly.

He said, "I know I am supposed to do this because I had a trip to Ohio planned, and it was canceled today. So if you don't mind, I will stand up on Sunday morning at my church and see if I can get some of the other men to come and help me." This particular Mennonite church already had a connection with our ministry because it was where Karen had held her baby dedication.

The following weekend, the men (and even some young boys) from his church came and put up every one of those walls in one day. The miracles do not stop there. A local countertop business donated countertops, and a few men volunteered to install them at the checkout counter. Someone brought a pressure washer and washed the outside of the store and the sidewalks. Friends, family, ministry partners, and board members started mopping floors, cleaning bathrooms, vacuuming rugs, and painting the walls for each alcove. Previous residents and a birthfather even joined us to help get the store ready for opening.

During this whirlwind of activity, I had gotten an estimate for cleaning the carpet—about $3,000—which was too steep for us. So I called another man to come and give me a quote. He came in and saw all the people working so hard and commented that we were putting a lot of money into this place to get it up and going. I replied, "No sir, all of these people are volunteering their time to help us out." He couldn't believe what he was seeing. When he looked around, there were people washing windows, pulling up tile in the bathrooms, installing countertops, building alcove spaces, and painting every corner of the building.

As he looked around, he responded, "You are not kidding, Ma'am. You got a lot of nice help happening here. You weren't lying when you said all these people are helping you. I am not believing this!" When I asked him what price he was thinking about charging us, he responded, "There is no way I could charge you. When do you think all these people will be out of here? I will come back and clean this carpet free of charge."

Another man, Mr. Smith, the former caretaker of the T.E Jones Furniture building, stopped by to see if we needed anything. I told him, "No, sir. But we have just been talking about how nice it would be to have music in the store." I then asked him if those speakers in the ceiling worked. He told me that they did work and asked if we wanted a CD player for them. I quickly replied, "Yes, that would be wonderful!" So he brought back the 36-disc CD changer that the furniture store had used. God had supplied again–this time, not exactly for a need but for a desire.

The Alcoves of A Place for Us Ministries opened on Black Friday of 2005. We had twenty-one brave vendors with faith enough to venture out on this calling along with us. We are forever thankful for all those who took that step of faith and for all those who are partnering with us still today.

Even More

Eventually, we were able to add our upscale resale boutique we call The Secret Place. All the items needed for both The Alcoves and The Secret Place had been donated by Elisse Sorrow, who had recently closed her boutique. She provided window displays, registers, fixtures, clothes, checkout counters, and even wrapping stations and accessories.

From the beginning, we wanted to have a Bible and book store inside The Alcoves. In 2009, with the failing economy, The Shepherd's Shoppe was forced to close their large store and downsize. They became an answer to our prayers when they moved in, bringing not only books and CD's but also other encouraging merchandise such as inspirational greeting cards, gifts, and home decor.

Another dream we had for the store was to have a tearoom. This dream was confirmed when Debbie Hite toured the building for the first time. She had been praying about opening up a tearoom. At this point, the building had been almost completely emptied out, but she discovered one lamp which had been left in the building; it was made out of a teapot. This was a confirmation for Debbie as well. However, she did not join us right away, but Rayne Adams felt led to come in and set up a café. Rayne and her husband Gene worked hard to get His Place Café up and running. Then they handed it over to the ministry as a gift. The ministry operated it while allowing some of our residents to work there and gain job skills. One of these residents later told us that working in the café while in our program had helped her gain the skills she needed to secure a job overseeing waitresses at a restaurant in her home town. In God's timing, Debbie came in and transformed the café into the Goodness and Mercy Tea Room. She operated it for a while but soon had to leave town to take care of her elderly parents. She sold her equipment to June and Bill Martin and their daughter Robin. Ms. June and Mr. Bill now run the tearoom, which has become known around the Greenwood area for its delicious food and peaceful lunch setting.

The Alcoves is more than just a mini-mall. It hosts a wide range of new upscale merchandise ranging from collegiate, designer clothing, gardening, and home décor to jewelry and much more. We have baby and bridal registries where soon-to-be parents or brides choose unique gifts for starting off these special seasons in their lives. People hear about this unique shopping experience and drive several hours from all over to come visit The Alcoves, "where shopping leads to hope." But more than being a wonderful place to shop, The Alcoves is a "light on a hill" for our community. We have a box for customers to place prayer requests in, and the staff prays with customers who desire prayer. Often, we hear testimonies of answered prayer or of God stories that happened in the store.

One story was about a lady who came into the store soon after losing her mother. Instead of sending flowers, a friend had given her a gift certificate to The Alcoves. As she browsed the booths, she came across one that carried antiques and unique china. She was pleasantly surprised to find china that was identical to her mother's, and they were the exact pieces she was missing from her mother's collection. The cost happened to be the exact amount on the gift certificate! She told one of the sales associates she felt this was a special gift from God just for her. She left that day with her china complete and her heart filled with a special sense of closeness to her mother. These stories and so many more have occurred inside the walls of The Alcoves. Many people have come in and felt God's amazing peace. Many others stop in just for lunch because they say that here they can have a quick lunch while feeling the closeness and peace of God.

God also had plans for the lower level that we never could have imagined. The basement now serves as a donation center for The Secret Place Boutique. There, items are sorted, steamed, tagged, and priced for the showroom floor. We also have our maternity closet and baby closet, which serve the needs of our residents and their babies. Another function of the lower level is to provide a place for the community to come together at a monthly prayer meeting hosted by Joe and Rachel Hill. On the first Monday night of the month, Joe Hill comes and shares a short message and prays with people that need hope and encouragement. We hear many testimonies from these meetings: people who have been without jobs for months have found jobs, people have been healed from all kinds of sickness and disease, and people have been delivered of drug and alcohol addiction. The Most Excellent Way, a Christ centered, Bible-honoring discipleship ministry dedicated to helping people receive and experience new life by faith in Jesus Christ, meets on the other Monday nights. Through these meetings led by Tommy and Bonnie Boyd, many who are struggling have experienced freedom from their addictive habits, destructive patterns, and the hurts that led to them.

God took our small vision of 1,000 square feet and turned it into His vision of 22,000 square feet. What we thought was impossible, God knew was possible. Our idea of the space we needed wasn't His idea of the space He knew we needed. From the beginning, He had the plan, and He saw each person who would come into this space and be changed. The Alcoves began as a small idea, but it has grown into more than a store. It is a marketplace ministry where people from all walks and stations can receive a personal touch from the Lord.

Sowing Seeds of Hope

A Vendor's Heart

by Suzanne Carroll

In you shall all the nations be blessed.
Galatians 3:8 ESV

November of 2005, Lesa Jefferies and I sensed that the Lord was leading us to rent a booth at The Alcoves. We discussed several different options for our booth, but nothing seemed to be the right fit. Then one day as Lesa was browsing through the internet, she came across a jewelry website. This jewelry was crafted in Israel by a Messianic Jew named Leehee.[1] The breathtaking designs were born out of Leehee's vision to touch and encourage people's hearts through God's Word. Inscribed on the pieces were Scriptures written in English, Hebrew, or both. Lesa was overwhelmed by them and was certain that God had led her there. She could hardly wait to tell me about it.

That evening the two of us, along with our husbands, headed out for a neighborhood walk. We had been in a routine of walking together; that was one way for us to be physically active in order to stay healthy. The walk down North Main Street usually took us down to Ingles and back to the town square. As we walked and talked, Lesa told me about the jewelry and that she believed God had surely directed her to it. As she spoke, my excitement grew, and I could not wait to get home and look up this amazing opportunity to share God's Word in such a unique way.

It was a cool evening in November, and the men had gained some distance as they walked ahead of us. We were about halfway to Ingles, still excitedly talking about this new venture, when we were both shocked to feel a warm, rushing wind. Wondering where this powerful, warm breeze had come from, I asked Lesa, "Did you feel that?" She **had** felt it and was equally puzzled by it. We called out to our husbands to see if they had felt it too; their answer was, "No." This warm breeze had hit us just as Lesa and I were discussing that this venture was not for us to profit from, but to enable us to do for others and help others in various ways. We tossed about different names as we tried to decide what to call our alcove. We decided that LeZanne's would be the perfect name—a combination of Lesa and Suzanne. With this opportunity before us, we committed to support A Place for Us Ministries and other ministries with the profits.

The next day, we encountered some obstacles when trying to contact Leehee on the internet. Computer glitches were preventing

Lesa from being able to contact her, so she contacted one of the stores that carried Leehee jewelry to try to get some more information. They gave her Leehee's e-mail address, but when Lesa e-mailed the company, she found out they were not accepting new customers at the time. Our hearts sank with this news because we had hoped to have our booth open before Christmas. Then the Lord intervened to remove the obstacles. The other store that carried Leehee jewelry allowed us to buy their overstock so that we could open our booth before Christmas.

Next, when Lesa went to the courthouse to apply for the business license, the ladies in that office were curious and asked if she had any pictures of the jewelry. She did, and when she showed them some of the jewelry pieces, they cried. Lesa was amazed to see them get so emotional over the jewelry and the way God's Word had spoken to them through these pictures. This encounter reminded her that "every part of Scripture is God-breathed and useful one way or another" (II Timothy 3:16 MSG). After she told me what had happened, we decided to e-mail Leehee to share the story and ask her to reconsider accepting LeZanne's as a new customer. We heard back from Leehee the very next day. She had been touched by our story and was willing to help. She sent us the products that she had left for the rest of the year to help us start the booth. She also told us about her new designs, which would be available after the first of the year. LeZanne's would soon become an active supplier of her designs. Lesa and I were overjoyed that in spite of the obstacles, a new journey of faith had begun.

Shortly after starting LeZanne's, I sat down at my computer and wrote a poem called "A Voice in the Wind."

A voice so small, was heard by two
On a path of concrete and stone.
This dusky autumn night had been prepared
God's direction would soon be shown.

Plans made by man, will not succeed
Confusion they will impart.

The wind of heaven is the one true voice
Listen to it, for a fresh new start.

The wind blew warm across our face
God's voice was heard so clear.
"I will establish your steps as you walk in faith
My Word, it will draw near."
Those lost and lonely will find in it
Hope, comfort, healing, and strength.
My song of mercy, life and love
Dear child, the depth, it knows no length.

That's it, we said and God's presence brought forth
A plan birth'd in the heavenly realm.
Scripture jewelry will speak to those willing to hear
God's truth and presence will draw them near.

Over the past six years, LeZanne's has carried several different lines of scripture jewelry and has blessed many lives, including ours. God's Spirit has touched men, women, and children, young and old, as they have stepped into LeZanne's to read His Word and perhaps purchase an item that will bring hope and peace to themselves or to their loved one. We have continued to honor our commitment to use the profits from LeZanne's to bless others. In addition to supporting A Place for Us Ministries above and beyond what is required as a vendor at The Alcoves, LeZanne's has supported several ministries around the world. We have supported a ministry in China's red-light district that is working to eliminate the sex-slave trade, a mission's ministry in Costa Rica, a ministry in Mozambique that recently led over five thousand people in one village to accept Jesus' invitation of salvation, and we have sowed into a ministry in Sudan. In fact, nearly one hundred percent of the profits from LeZanne's have been donated to ministries that are sowing seeds of hope and restoration, both in the community and around the world.

More Than the ABC's

The Learning Center Story
by Lesa Jefferies

Do not forget my teaching,
but keep my commands in your heart,
for they will prolong your life many years
and bring you peace and prosperity
Proverbs 3:1-2 NIV

E laine Hall, a frequent shopper at the newly opened store, The Alcoves, began to learn about the ministry and became very interested in the fact that we wanted to give the residents of APFU an opportunity to learn more than what would be learned at just a typical day at school. One of the things that appealed to her was that she knew we desired to teach Biblical studies to the residents as well as educational studies. She was very interested in helping because she learned that the majority of our girls end up choosing to parent their children and need to know how to manage a checkbook, a household, and so much more. The vision for a learning center was something the board had foreseen since inception. We felt as though each girl coming through the program needed more than just a high school diploma. They needed to be taught in-depth classes on submission to authority, anger management, nutrition, budgeting, parenting, adoption education, career planning, resume writing and much more. There were many resources that we had collected over the years, and we were ready to put a program together that each girl would benefit from. It is a privilege to come to APFU and have access to valuable classes being taught.

Often we are able to access volunteers who will come in and teach classes. Elaine became a valuable volunteer who would do just that. Soon 327 Cardinal Lane was planned out and up and running. The inspiration for the name came out of hours of prayer-walking in the basement. The number 327 represents Proverbs 3:27, "Do not withhold good from those to whom it is due, when it is in your power to act" (NIV). Little by little, with Elaine arranging the previously donated desks and conference tables plus a few added touches from the decorative flair of a few Alcove vendors, the Learning Center became a cozy atmosphere where the girls would attend classes four days a week. Elaine even volunteered her time to teach the classes and still to this day supports APFU through prayer and in other ways as needed. Elaine explained it this way:

This verse seemed to be the life goal of the cardinal. They minister to each other and to humans. They set an example of doing what you can (what is in your power or resources) for someone along the journey of life. As girls come to the Learning Center,

God provides the resources to meet their needs for that part of their journey. The Learning Center is not a place for just education. It is a place to nurture the physical, mental, and spiritual needs of the soul that enters. It is a place of relationship building by meeting needs and then journeying closer to Christ.

As God revealed the initial design and the needs, He would send the resources. People came and would donate or do decorating that fit with what He revealed. Resources came as different ones were led to do what was in their power to do. Many miles seemed to be walked in that basement praying for the physical structure and the ministry that was to take place...all the time knowing this was to be a temporary shelter from the life storms—a place for visitors to gain their footing, walk at a slower pace for awhile and make choices regarding life.

In 2010, a resident battling many life-controlling issues noticed the cardinals on the walls and other places when she first came into the Learning Center. Thinking they must have some kind of meaning, she looked it up for herself. Learning that the cardinal is a sign of protection and hearing the story behind 327 Cardinal Lane really ministered to her.

A New Beginning

Eventually we were able to hire a Learning Center Program Coordinator, Sally Jayne Acosta. Sally Jayne loves God and loves God's Word. She implemented really wonderful lessons and activities while on staff. One special thing that Sally Jane did for the girls was inspired by something God had placed on the heart of one of our volunteers several years prior. Jessica was a volunteer who instantly fell in love with our mission and our residents. Inspired by Max Lucado's book, *A Love Worth Giving*, Jessica bought herself a pinky ring as a reminder that God never gives up on us. It meant so much to her that she wanted to do the same for the residents. She bought them all pinky rings to remind them that God loves them, still believes in them, and has good plans for them.

Years later, Sally Jayne came across a sterling silver filigree ring that symbolized new beginnings. She felt this ring would be perfect for our residents to receive when they graduate the program. She and her husband started purchasing these rings for the girls. When they moved away, they decided to continue the tradition, so they still provide our residents with the beautiful new beginnings ring. Each of our graduates from the program receives this ring, and they all seem to love and appreciate its symbolism that God transforms the old into a new beginning. We think it is important to make graduation a monumental event. Many of these girls have given up so much to come into the program and try to get the help that they need. We celebrate their completion by hosting a graduation celebration. The residents are able to invite their friends and family. We show a video of their journey while at A Place for Us, and they are given their ring and a special note from Sally Jayne and her husband. Bonnie also blesses the girls with a scrapbook of their journeys to keep and remember the ways God has worked in their lives while at A Place for Us.

For Such a Time as This

After Sally Jayne and her husband moved, we needed a Learning Center Program Coordinator again. This time, God would use miraculous means to show us His choice. Since our inception, Sherri and her husband Mike have been supporters of A Place for Us Ministries. Sherri had always desired to serve actively in the ministry but had been unable to do so because she was the primary caregiver for her husband's grandmother, who suffered from Alzheimer's. However, in June of 2009, Mike's grandmother had to be placed in a long-term care facility, so Sherri was now available.

Having heard of this job opening, Sherri began to wonder if this was her time to join the ministry. She knew that she had the experience and the organizational skills necessary to handle the day-to-day regimen of the Learning Center. However, there were many things to consider about this job—one being the great job that she already had at a local hospital. The fact that they offered her a substantial raise shortly after she applied for the APFU job might have thrown her off a bit. However, after discussing it with her husband, Sherri knew that applying for the job was the step that God had wanted her to take.

During the interview, it was very clear to the board that she was passionate about helping young women and seeing their lives changed through the power of Jesus Christ. Sherri prayed and prayed about the job, asking God to show her if she was just being overly eager or if He was changing her line of work for His purposes.

Many employees who have joined the ministry have come to us through seemingly supernatural means. The Lord would give them signs or show them something that would solidify their decision to work with A Place for Us. For Sherri, it was no different. This account is in Sherri's own words.

One night I had a dream, which I believe was from the Lord. In this dream, I saw alcove sections with palm trees all around and one palm tree particularly sitting at the bottom of the steps of this temple, which resembled a palace. There were outer courts and inner courts, and all of it was so beautiful and majestic. But the thing that really stood out to me the most were the towering beautiful palm trees in every nook and corner. Earlier in the week, prior to the dream, I had read Ezekiel chapter 40. That morning when I had awakened, I was led back to those passages. The words on the page matched my dream almost identically. I did not know why at the time, but I sincerely felt that this dream was linked somehow to both mine and the board's confirmation that I would be the one for the job. I did not share the dream with anyone; however I did call my friend Lesa, the Director at A Place for Us, and told her that I had a dream and just couldn't figure out if it meant anything concerning the job there at the ministry. While sharing the dream with her, I told her that I felt that she needed to go into the Learning Center and see if there were any palm trees. Lesa quickly said that she already knew that there were palm trees, one silk palm tree and two pictures of palm trees. At this point Lesa was beginning to see a connection with the dream that I did not know a thing about. I then told her that in my dream, I was told to go find the "palm tree." Lesa exclaimed, "Tammie is the palm tree!" It startled me to hear her excitement and confused me as well. Earlier in the week, unbeknownst to me, Tammie had been given a palm tree figurine from Bonnie Boyd. Bonnie had a book about the Hebrew meaning of names. In the book she had found that Tammie's name meant Tamara which meant palm tree, strength, and wisdom. Lesa exclaimed, "I don't know why God has given you that dream, but Tammie is the one that God is leading you to!"

The Lord continued confirming His call in Sherri's heart through little things as she continued to wait for an answer, and the ministry continued to pray about whom to hire since they had not yet come to a final decision. About a week later, the board decided that the other applicant was the one for the job, so they made her an offer. Tammie knew that God was in control, and if this lady accepted the offer, then she was His choice. However, she still wondered about Sherri and if she was the one God had chosen for the job. In the meantime, while the other applicant was praying about the offer the ministry had given her, Tammie began to pray for both applicants. Through God's Word, He kept reminding Tammie that it was all about the heart. This of course was not to say that the other applicant's heart was not right. This was all about hiring the right person for the season that the ministry was in at the time. "There is a time for everything and a season for every activity under heaven" (Ecclesiastes 3:1 NIV). The Lord just kept showing Tammie some things that were important for the person that we were to hire, so she felt led to ask Sherri about her favorite Bible character. She had me to email Sherri and ask her the question. That night, I dreamed that I had gone to Sherri and asked her the question personally, and her answer was Elijah. I didn't remember from the dream why Sherri had responded with Elijah, but driving to work the next morning, I wondered if the dream was going to be a confirmation. Below is Sherri's account of her answer.

It was funny when I received the email asking me who my favorite Bible character was because my seventeen-year-old son had just asked me the very same question that morning. I thought it was really strange to receive an email asking this question again. However, my answer was the same as what I had told my son just hours earlier–Elijah. I chose Elijah because of his bold faith, especially when opposition came against his passion for his purpose to proclaim his heart for God.

I was simply amazed when I opened up my email the next morning and read the word *Elijah* on my computer screen. It gave me a peace about the decision, so I shared my dream and Sherri's answer with Tammie. However, Elijah was not the character that Tammie had in her mind. Tammie's Bible reading had been about David and his heart, so she had been hoping that Sherri's answer would be *David*. She continued to pray, and the next day, she read more in her study Bible about the heart, and there was a section about Elijah and his heart for God and His people. Tammie couldn't believe what she was reading, but she now knew that Sherri was the one God really wanted for the job. However, the board had already offered the job to another wonderful, well-qualified woman. When Sherri learned that the job had been filled, she was very disappointed. She still told Tammie that she trusted what God had shown her and the board, and she knew the Lord would use her to serve in some other capacity at A Place for Us Ministries. Sherri cried many tears over the decision because she had felt so strongly that this was what the Lord was calling her to do. However, she accepted it and continued working at her other job.

As it turned out, the other woman was unable to take the position. The board of directors met again, and after hearing all the confirmations from both Tammie and me, they decided to offer the job to Sherri, which she gladly accepted. No one was sure why God orchestrated things the way He did, but we trusted that God had a purpose behind it. Maybe it was to show us that even if we make a wrong decision while trusting His guidance, God will accomplish His purposes. In this case, He knew that Sherri was the perfect one for the next few steps of our journey.

From the beginning of the ministry, the board of directors had a vision to serve girls facing situations other than unplanned pregnancies. When several board members visited Mercy Ministries, the Holy Spirit confirmed their vision and showed them that the reason they were named A Place for Us Ministries was that there would be more than one ministry. Throughout the years, the subject of opening the doors of the home to other troubled girls would come up, but the timing was never right.

Sherri brought this issue back into the forefront when she presented a desperate situation to the board. A young teenager in an extreme crisis needed immediate intervention. The board prayed about the situation and unanimously agreed that it was time to open the doors to girls who find themselves facing many different crises—including eating disorders, self harm, unhealthy relationships, substance abuse, and more.

In addition to rescuing this teenage girl, Sherri's leadership became vital in keeping everything going smoothly after the "unexpected turn" in Tammie's journey. Sherri took charge, working far beyond her job description or paid hours, serving the girls and the other staff. We are truly grateful that God sent Sherri to us for that season of the ministry. Sherri's greatest quote for the girls at the Learning Center was, "Every choice leads you somewhere"—a very true saying, not only for the girls but for us as well.

Forever Changed

Every Learning Center Program Coordinator needs an assistant—someone to help with the daily activities and classes at the Learning Center. Sally Jayne had Elaine to help her. Sherri had Ms Shirley. Ms. Shirley was a great help to Sherri, but it turned out that she received our help as well.

Ms. Shirley was hired at A Place for Us through the Experience Works program sponsored by the One Stop Employment office. This program was designed to help workers over the age of fifty-five to find employment after the plants where they had originally been employed closed down. Here is Ms. Shirley's story in her own words:

I grew up in a home with six siblings, both of my parents, and my grandmother. We had a very loving home, and my parents kept us in church and taught us about the Lord. At that time, I felt I had a good relationship with God.

I attended public school and graduated from Brewer High School in 1970. After high school, I went to Piedmont Technical College to major in Textile Management. I didn't get to finish working on my degree because I started working third shift at Greenwood Mills #5 plant. As time went on, I started to date a young man named William who I affectionately call "Bug." On June 19, 1976, we got married in Bug's uncle's house. His uncle was a Baptist minister. One year later, we had our son and only child, Carl.

Our marriage wasn't the best because Bug liked to hang in the streets with his friends. My son and I would be at home alone or at my parent's house while Bug chose the "street life." He would come home most times between 1:00 and 1:30 a.m. on the weekends. He never really hung out through the week because of work. He was a great provider. However, when he hung out in the streets, he would come home drunk. Eventually, his drinking led to physical abuse towards my son and me.

After six years of physical abuse from my husband, I moved to my parents' house with our son because I could not take the abuse any longer. My son and I were physically and emotionally broken. I felt we needed that time apart to regroup. I was tired and didn't know if I wanted our marriage to continue.

In October of 1986, I moved into my own apartment with my son. My husband started to come over to see us and eventually moved back in with us in 1989. At first, he did really well. Eventually, he returned to the pattern of his old behaviors. I had to give him a choice: his buddies and the street life or his family. He stayed and stopped smoking, but He didn't really change his "street life."

In 1994, I became severely ill with pneumonia and thyroid issues. This made me realize how much I needed a closer relationship with God. I had fallen away from my walk with Christ because I allowed my issues with Bug to consume me. About a year later, I recommitted my life to the Lord. Over the years, my health continued to decline.

Despite my health issues, I still had to work, and in 1984, I was transferred to Matthews Mill. Bug came to work there as well in the following year in 1985. He would often come to work with a hangover because of his "street life," and I would end up helping him with his job. I really had to because if he got fired, it would not only affect him, but it would affect my son and me.

In December 2006, I received a letter saying that Mathews Mill would be closing their doors in February of 2007. When that time came, my whole department was out of jobs. Bug's floor was allowed to remain until August of 2007, when they closed the plant completely.

I went to the One Stop employment office to receive my unemployment benefits after I was let go from the plant. One day, as I was going into their office, I saw a flyer advertising a new program that was in a place called Experience Works. This program helped people over the age of fifty-five seek employment and job training skills. Ms. Martha Patterson at that office helped me find the job at A Place for Us Ministries. At first, I was afraid to go to A Place for Us Ministries because I only had experience in textiles. When I went to my interview with Ms. Tammie, there was a peace that I felt when I talked to her. I spoke about this job with my family, and they encouraged me to give it a shot.

I knew right away that this place was unique and different. There were times when I would come into work not feeling well, and they would stop what they were doing just to pray for me. I learned to love the young ladies and staff at this ministry because I was still dealing with the situation with Bug which *caused me to have hatred toward him. At some points, I felt like giving up. However, the Bible studies and the prayers that they prayed for Bug encouraged me to keep going, and my faith was slowly strengthened.*

As I continued to receive encouragement daily from the staff at APFU, my heart was still heavy because Bug had not changed. He was an abusive alcoholic. In 2010 something changed. Bug got sick. He was having panic attacks and was thinking about committing suicide. One day, he went outside of our house for a while. I wasn't sure what was bothering him and why he was feeling uneasy. When he came back into the house, he did something that totally surprised me and Carl. He asked us if we would forgive him for the things he had done to us all these years. We both told him that we had already forgiven him. I knew that this was God working on his heart because of the prayers that had been offered up on his behalf by the ladies at the Learning Center.

In September 2010, he went to the doctor and was informed that he had diabetes. Immediately, he stopped drinking! I knew it was the prayers! Shortly after that, he accepted Christ into his life! He reads his Bible now and writes scriptures from the Bible and focuses on how to apply them to his life. He has started mentoring other guys to let them know that they need to give their lives to Christ. He boldly shares his testimony with them to let them know that he has walked the same path they are walking, but God changed him. He attends church often, and every time I go, he attends church with me.

If it were not for the prayers and support of the women at the Learning Center and APFU staff, I don't know if he would have ever given his life to Christ. I thank God for this ministry.

Ms. Shirley says that we benefited her, but we have certainly been blessed by her as well. Ms. Shirley has such a great personality, and when she gives the girls a speech, residents and staff alike enjoy her unique way of getting her point across, a lesson we won't easily forget. There has not been one girl who has gone through our program that has not fallen in love with Ms. Shirley and her hilarious teaching style. She teaches them in a way that they can receive it—not preachy or demanding and usually mixed with a healthy dose of laughter. One such "speech" is how she tells the girls to remain pure after leaving our program. She uses the example of a pocket book. She says, "If you don't want other people's spare change inside your pocketbook, then you need to keep it closed." Sometimes the girls don't get it right away, but when Ms. Shirley leans over and looks them wide-eyed, square in their faces and whispers what she means by their "pocketbook," the girls usually erupt in laughter. We are certain that the girls never forget the "pocketbook" example!

We have been amazed how each time God brings someone new to the Learning Center, it expands our vision to catch a greater glimpse of God's original plan. It keeps getting better and better each year as we grow and learn what the residents need as they face the challenges of this life. And that is why the story matters.

The Wilted Pansy—Still Hope Remains

Kate's Story

The grass withers and the flowers fade,
but the word of our God stands forever
Isaiah 40:8 NLT

Bonnie's Perspective:

I am Bonnie Boyd, a sales associate at The Alcoves. I remember very clearly the first day that I met Kate. To me it is always a good day at The Alcoves when I am able to take time with one or two customers to pray with them or speak an encouraging word to them. Many times the Lord allows me the privilege of encouraging people by sharing a book that might help them with something they are facing. The Shepherd's Shoppe is located within The Alcoves, so it is very easy to send someone there to find a book that might meet a need they have.

Although this was not Kate's first trip into The Alcoves, it was the first time she and I connected. It seems like yesterday, but it was almost two years ago that I was serving a beautiful, petite young lady with dark blonde, medium-length hair and big, pretty brown eyes. More than her countenance or her physical appearance, I noticed the book she was buying, *Boundaries.* I recognized it right away because I had my own copy, which I had read and had written notes all throughout its pages. That book had spoken to me life-changing truth that I needed to hear but would not have received from any person who tried to tell me. This truth was that I needed healthy boundaries within my marriage. I told her, "This book saved my marriage." At this time, I did not realize that this one simple comment would lead to a lasting friendship with this special young lady. It is such a joy to see Kate coming into the store. She always has the joy of the Lord bubbling over and a smile that is contagious. She is hungry for the things of God. It has blessed me to watch her grow in her relationship with God through the years. I have seen her weather the storms in her life and come out stronger on the other side.

Kate's Story:

As a little girl, I loved my Barbie dolls and watching movies of fairy tales. I could imagine Prince Charming coming to rescue me and take me away. In my early years, our family attended church occasionally. When I was eleven years old, I accepted Jesus into my heart and was baptized. I came to this decision mainly because of the influence of one particular Sunday school teacher. She was an inspiration to me; I could tell that she really loved the Lord, and that enthusiasm rubbed off on me. Her relationship with the Lord made me want to know more about Jesus. Unfortunately, she was asked to step down from her teaching position because she was going through a divorce. I was devastated. With this loss, disappointment and confusion crept in, causing me to lose heart; and I fell away from God.

Around this time, my parents were growing more distant from each other. When I was in middle school, my parents announced that they were going to separate. I cried so hard that they changed their minds and decided to stay together. Things seemed to go back to normal in our family. I guess they were just good at hiding things because it all looked good on the outside, but that wasn't the case. When I was in high school, my mom caught my father having an affair, and the marriage ended that day. I will never forget the moment my world came crashing down when she told me. This time, I realized that they really were going through with the divorce, and nothing I could do would change the situation. I was forced to grow up fast at this point. Now, instead of being shielded from the family drama, I was right in the middle of it. No child should have to go through this. Even through all the drama, I still managed to play tennis, participate in the class beauty pageants, and become class president; but along with the roles I was playing in school, I had another new role at home. Instead of being a daughter, I became more like a friend. Somehow, I continued to have a great relationship with both parents while trying in my own way to help them both heal.

After high school, I became a pharmaceutical sales representative. I was a single, working woman who was still waiting for my knight with his bright and shining armor to come and steal me away. Over the past few years, the upheaval caused by my parents' divorce had been shaping and re-defining my own dreams and boundaries. Along the way, I had resolved that I would not marry until I found a man with whom I felt confident I could build a strong marriage. However, my "knight in shining armor" soon appeared on the scene and started charming his way past my re-defined boundaries. James came into my world and swept me off my feet—but not with his looks. (It's not that he was bad looking; he was tall, with a cute boyish face, blue eyes, and blonde hair.) It was his irresistible charm and fantastic personality that drew me to him. He pursued me like I had never been pursued before. James always told me how wonderful I was and that he could have had anyone he wanted, but he chose me. I always took that as a compliment. Charming, likeable, funny, and very social, he liked being the center of attention. All these things attracted me to James, and I began to fall head over heels in love with him.

After we dated for a year and a half, we moved in together. Looking back, I realize that I had based many of my decisions on a lie. I thought if James and I lived together, it would be a good way to make sure we were right for each other before making a commitment to marriage. I felt it would prove to me that our marriage would last. I see now how choosing to live together first really doesn't work. If you do feel that person is not right for you, you have already invested so much time in that person and relationship that it seems crazy to back out. One of you has already given up your home, your family already expects you to be together, and you have already persevered through so many challenges. Staying with that person just ends up feeling like the right thing to do.

If living together wasn't enough to prove to me that I could marry James and be confident that our marriage would last, I also used another test. I studied his parents. I closely analyzed their marriage, hoping to find a stable relationship. I assumed that after the "*I do*'s," my marriage to James would be a carbon copy of what I saw in his parents' marriage. I guess I believed we passed all my tests because after living together about a year, we decided to get married. Finally, my dream had come true; I was married to my Prince Charming. We were happy, and we soon got the news that we were going to be "Mommy" and "Daddy."

No, I am not one of the clients of A Place for Us Ministries. I didn't have to make a desperate phone call, needing a place to stay because I was pregnant and homeless. But I **am** someone whose life was touched and changed by God through their ministry. My job as a sales rep brings me into Greenwood on a regular basis. I had heard about The Alcoves by word of mouth. Finally, on one of my trips, I decided to stop in to see what it was all about. From then on, it became a favorite place for me to visit while in town. I would often stop in to have lunch in the Tea Room and browse through the store. I didn't know why when I first started going there, but I knew that the atmosphere in this place was different. There was something special about the place. It was so peaceful and inviting, like Grandma's house.

One day, while in The Tea Room, I just happened to look over at the shelves in the Shepherd's Shoppe and spotted a Bible on CD. I remembered how I had always wanted to read the entire Bible. I thought, "I could buy it on CD and listen to it while I'm traveling on my job." So I bought it and began listening to it in my car. At this point, my life was perfectly vanilla; I had a good job, a wonderful husband, and a son I adored with all my heart. Now I was enjoying traveling with the Bible on CD and having conversations with people about what I was learning.

When I made that purchase, I had no idea that God had planned it to prepare me for what was ahead. By the time I had made it to the book of Isaiah, my life turned upside down. The night after my son's second birthday party, a wife's worst nightmare played out in my real life. James had not come home, and I was worried sick. I thought at any moment, I would get a call from someone telling me that he was dead. He had gone out with one of his friends. Finally, he came home at four in the morning—with a very attractive woman. He claimed she was his ride since he had been drinking. He let her come into the house to use our bathroom and then walked her to her car. In the long minutes I stood waiting for him to come back into the house, relief and fear and dread all molded together to form a clump in my chest. I went out to see why it was taking him so long and found him kissing her. Although it was April, and the grass was green, and leaves were budding on the trees, in that moment, everything in my life turned dark, cold, and gray.

From that moment on, my life became a roller coaster ride from disappointment to hope to disappointment to despair. James agreed to go to counseling. Then, one month into the counseling, he insisted on moving into an apartment while we worked on our marriage issues. I found out that, in addition to that one night fling with another woman, he was also addicted to pornography. But we were working on these things in counseling. I believed that things would get better, and James would get the help he needed.

Struggling to keep my world from unraveling, I was going through the motions, trying to work and be a mom but was crashing on the inside. I still listened to my Bible on CD while I worked my route. That Word became a healing ointment to my heart and gave me strength for each new day. Although my life and marriage were in shambles, God was doing a work within me. I began to give Him my whole heart for the first time. I also continued visiting The Alcoves on my lunch break when my schedule took me to Greenwood.

When God first led me to The Alcoves, He knew that in the near future, I would need the comfort and encouragement of godly people in my life, and He knew exactly where to send me. Looking back now, I know the day I met Bonnie Boyd had to be one of those God things because my last intention was to go in and start a conversation about my failing marriage. I was very private about my husband's issues, and I did not want to say anything that would make him look bad. However, at this point, I was just so weary of trying to carry the burden alone, and I was willing to grasp any lifeline within sight. The book on boundaries seemed to be a good start. I was doing my best to lean on the Lord, but sometimes you just need to talk to someone who has been in your shoes and survived. It all started when Bonnie saw the book I had picked up at the Shepherd's Shoppe. You can imagine my initial shock followed by a wave of hope rippling through me when she said, "That book saved my marriage." She took the time to share her story with me—about her husband's addiction to prescription drugs and how it had almost destroyed their marriage and family. Then she told of how God had delivered him from this addiction and restored their marriage. Now He was using them to reach out to others. She also recommended that I read *Power of a Praying Wife*, by Stormie Omartian. Deeply encouraged after hearing her story, I felt my hope was renewed. She prayed with me and left me with a phone number of a Mr. Joe Hill—someone for me to call if I wanted special prayer.

After my lunch break, I went on to see my next client, Dr. Hill. I always loved making this stop because Dr. Hill and I would usually talk about God, and he would ask me what book of the Bible I was listening to now. He would answer any questions I had. I was always encouraged by our conversations. Well, this afternoon, I told him about "this lady" I had met at The Alcoves and how she had given me a number to call for someone to pray for me. I was about to ask him what he thought about it when I realized that he had the same last name. I thought he must be the one Bonnie had meant. I asked, "Are you the one she told me to call?"

He laughed, and said, "No, but that is my dad." That was a very cool God moment. It was one of those meant-to-be moments in my life. I needed so desperately to see God at work, and He didn't disappoint me. It seemed each time I visited The Alcoves, God continued to build relationships that I would need to help me weather the storm.

I also grew to love the owners of the Goodness and Mercy Tearoom, Mr. Bill and Ms. June. They are like the all-American model for grandparents. They nurtured me with encouraging words and lifted me up in prayer each time I stopped in for lunch. As my visits increased, I also became close friends with some of the frequent customers and diners at The Alcoves and many times would have lunch with them. Through The Alcoves, God so graciously connected me with a godly support group that played a vital role in helping me through some very difficult situations.

Still in counseling but living separate lives, James and I could not move forward this way. He had been in the apartment for three months, and I sensed that things still were not right with him, but I had no proof for my suspicions. I told him that if he wanted to stay in this marriage, he could not live separate from us in the apartment. At first, he chose the apartment, but after a week he decided to come back home and canceled his contract on the apartment. Here I was—doing all I knew to do to mend our broken marriage, still hoping somehow this would all go away, and it would all work out—that it would turn out to be just a bad dream. One month later, he went on a weekend camping trip to get away by himself. When he came home, I found a key card for a hotel among his things. When

I confronted him, he said he had gotten tired of camping because it was raining and went to a hotel. After this, I couldn't shake the feeling that there was another woman. All these months, I had been trying to believe his excuses, but this time there seemed to be something inside of me showing me that he was living a lie. His words and his actions did not match up.

All of this was even harder to swallow because over the years, James and I had talked about adultery, and we had decided that before one of us ever decided to look outside the marriage for satisfaction, we would first walk away from the marriage. We had agreed that the hurt and the pain that came with adultery was something neither of us ever wanted to experience. I had never felt insecure in our marriage because he told me often that I was the only one for him, and I believed him. There had been times when he would show signs of being jealous, and when that happened, I always honored him and would keep my relationships with the opposite sex on a business level only. But now, I just could not shake this sick feeling inside me. He still would not admit that he was being unfaithful when I questioned him. I continued to seek counsel and prayer about what to do. In the meantime, I was keeping my peace through the Lord, His Word, church, and fellowship with other believers. I even purchased the book *Power of a Praying Wife*. I wanted my marriage to be saved; I wanted our son to have a family. Through this storm, I began to realize that many times I had made my husband and our relationship an idol. I decided then, that with or without James, it was time to put God first in my life. When I decided to change and put God first, God began giving me the strength I needed to face my trials.

I wanted to trust James, but because his words and actions did not line up, I knew in my heart that I could not believe him. So I decided to hire a private investigator. After the PI caught him with another woman, he still denied that he was having an affair. As my world was falling apart, I asked him to leave. There were many days when I couldn't even get out of bed. Every emotion you can think of, I experienced it. I even thought of what and how many pills I could take just to end the whole nightmare. I wanted to become a recluse. I had friends who had to call me sometimes to tell me to get out of bed and go to work. I could hardly function; I did not have energy to do anything. Even though I was not the one in the sin, I still somehow felt guilty. I can't really explain this, but it was there. I felt like when people looked at me, they were saying, "There is Kate; she is getting a divorce because her husband is having an affair." I felt they were wondering, "What did she do or not do to make her husband want another woman?" I cannot explain the guilt and shame that I wore like a heavy, dark cloak.

Through much soul-searching and prayer, I decided to forgive James and try to make things work. He came back home in October, but the drama continued as he continued to hide things from me for the next two months. Finally, it was taken out of my hands when the day after Christmas, James admitted that there was another woman (not the one in the car that night). He said he had strong feelings for her and was leaving me for her. With such devastating news, I cannot explain the peace that I felt. It was almost a sense of relief because now I no longer had to try to decide what to do. Just a few months earlier, I had been overwhelmed by despair and paralyzed by depression, but the day after Christmas, Jesus gave me a "peace that passes all understanding"(Philippians 4:7 AKJV).

This has been a hard road to travel, and the only way I am still traveling on it is through the grace of God and being in His Word. Honestly, if I go over one or two days without reading the Word, I can feel that anxiety and fear wanting to seep in. So my best advice to others facing this in your own life is to stay in the Word. Even at first, when the Bible may not even make sense, and you may not understand what you are reading, keep reading it anyway, and soon the Holy Spirit will begin to help you understand it, and it will change your life forever. It won't change the facts of different struggles you will face, but it will help you face them with a different attitude and have peace through the storms of this life.

With the divorce came the difficult challenge of setting up visitation between my son and his father. I have to say that I am very thankful that after the separation, James actually became a more attentive dad and—I guess you could say—a better father. I do believe that the "best father" is the one who has chosen first to be the best husband, honoring his child's mother. He has failed in that category, but I now call him the Disneyland Dad. He takes him to do all sorts of fun things all the time, and they have a ball. The really hard part is when you get a break from parenting, but it is not when you choose to have it but when it is mandated. It is especially hard when this was never your choice in the first place. I am thankful, though, that James does spend time with our son, even though he chose to abandon the family. It is hard, but I can't try to control what he does with our son when he has him. What I do that helps me is to think of it as if he is with his grandparents when they are keeping him. I know they love him but are obviously not going to do everything the way I would. This has become the new norm for my family, although not by my choice. I have to choose to be like Peter and keep my eyes on Jesus and not my circumstance, because when I take them off of Jesus, I begin to sink into the rough waters (Matthew 14:22-33). I am thankful that I have never wanted to retaliate, and I know that this is because I have stayed in the Word, and Jesus is doing this through me.

I would advise anyone going through a divorce not to enter into a relationship with the opposite sex for at least one year. You have to have time to heal; if not, you will be hurt again, or you will hurt the other person. One last note for anyone who is facing the issue of confronting and dealing with your spouse in areas of addiction, abuse, or adultery—remember that trust is earned—not just given! The one thing I feel that I could have done differently is to have drawn boundaries earlier on. I became a *wilted pansy* in my marriage. I should have found ways to express my thoughts, opinions, and feelings on things that really mattered and to stand up for them. I still believe in marriage; I know that it is still a beautiful covenant between a man and a woman.

I wish I could say that all the turmoil that I experienced over that year was the last of my heartache and trials for a while, but that is not the case. A year later, a new storm arose that would impact my life forever. Another visit to Greenwood and I stopped in at The Alcoves for lunch with friends. I enjoy every chance I get to spend a few hours re-connecting with my "second family." At some point, I realized that I had left my cell phone in my car, so I went out to check my messages. It was then that I saw a message from one of my mom's friends, asking me to call her back as soon as I could. I am so thankful that God had me get this message while I was at The Alcoves where I had the support of Christian friends. When I returned the call, she said that my mom was unresponsive, EMS was working with her, and she was on her way to Mom's house. She told me that she would call me back when she got there. Fear and confusion swirled around in my head. I went back into the tearoom and told my friends about the call. We prayed. Within minutes, I received the call that my mom was dead; they believed it was suicide. Shocked and dazed, I cried while my body shook. Devastated, questions flooded my mind. Quickly the news spread throughout the store, and I had a circle of friends gathering around me to pray for me and comfort my broken heart. I am so thankful for Mr. Bill and Ms. June who sat with me and consoled me until they were sure that I was stable enough to drive back home. I am also grateful for the special friends who drove over an hour to attend my mother's funeral. During the days and weeks that followed, I experienced God's amazing comfort and strong arms holding me up, just as it says in Isaiah 41:10: "So do not fear, for I am with you. Do not be dismayed, for I am your God. I will strengthen you and help you. I will uphold you with My righteous right hand" (NIV).

As devastating as it was to lose my mom to suicide, I can still honestly say that the divorce was the hardest thing I have ever faced. I know that I would never have chosen the circumstances that brought me to where I am today, but I am glad that they have led me on this journey with the Lord. He is the only one who can truly comfort me and heal my broken heart. I know God allowed my suffering to draw me close to Him so I could learn to rely on Him and not on other people or things. I am glad I did not have to travel this road alone; Jesus was there every step of the way. Romans 5:3-5 says, "And not only that, but we also glory in tribulations, knowing that tribulation produces perseverance; and perseverance, character; and character, hope. Now hope does not disappoint, because the love of God has been poured out in our hearts by the Holy Spirit who was given to us" (NKJV). These verses describe where I am today. I have hope in the midst of the storms, and I know that no disappointment, broken dream, or earthly circumstance is big enough to pluck me out of God's hands. Not long before my mom's death, I was praying at church for one of my cousins whose mother was dying of Lou Gehrig's disease. I remember telling my cousin, "God doesn't promise us a wonderful life; He promises us a wonderful ending." Once these words left my mouth, I knew that they were profound words from the Lord.

God doesn't promise us a wonderful life....
....He promises us a wonderful ending!

My name is Kate...and my story matters.

The Most Excellent Way

Zach's Story

For I am about to do something new.
See, I have already begun! Do you not see it?
I will make a pathway through the wilderness.
I will create rivers in the dry wasteland.
Isaiah 43:19 NLT

Tommy Boyd's Perspective (Leader of The Most Excellent Way*):

After suffering for years from the effects of addiction in my own life, I now invite others in similar situations to attend the meetings. Along my journey, I have learned that Christ has to be in the center of everyone's recovery plan. He is the only way I stay clean, so I enjoy sharing that with others. After numerous back surgeries, I became addicted to prescription drugs and abused them. Although my drugs did not come from the streets, I felt all the effects of drugs, I almost died, and I lost my family for a season. I finally chose to go into detox, and by the grace of God, He spared my life. Now I have to choose daily to stay clean.

For over three years now, each Monday, shortly after I arrive at The Alcoves to set up for the meetings, in comes Zach. He is there ready to learn and share what recovery means to him. I first met Zach at the Faith Home, a Christian-based rehab residential program where I was speaking to the men who are there in recovery. Zach had only been there two or three days when I met him. He listened very intently to what I had to say; I could tell he was very humbled as the tears rolled down his face. Later that day, I shared with him about The Most Excellent Way. He seemed very interested and said that he hoped to join us after graduating from Faith Home. That is exactly what Zach did, and he has been an asset to the meetings ever since. He is a very likeable young man. He is friendly and outgoing but handles himself in a quiet-like manner. If I had to describe Zach with three words, it would be "attitude of gratitude."

It is a privilege to be a part of Zach's story—to hear where he came from and to see his life now is an encouragement to me and to many others. Through his story, you will not only be encouraged to know there is freedom from addiction, but you will also be encouraged to never give up on people. As Zach shares his life story with you, you will hear how many wanted to give up on him. Thank the Lord they didn't because now God is using Zach to give back and help others. He not only attends The Most Excellent Way, but more often than not, he is bringing someone with him or lifting someone else up in prayer or speaking words of encouragement to others at the meetings.

Zack's Perspective

I grew up as an only child. My parents got a divorce when I was nine. It wasn't long before my mother re-married, and I lived with her and my stepfather. Right off the bat, I resented my stepfather. I really didn't have a just cause to dislike him, but that was just how I handled all the lies that my father made up about him and my mom. Around this time, I went to a Baptist summer camp. I had gone to church with my parents sometimes; so I knew about God. But the picture that I had of God was of a punishing God–watching to see if I messed up so He could zap me. I had heard sermons about hell and that if I didn't get saved, I would burn in hell. So, at this camp, I went to the front and prayed to ask Jesus into my heart. I didn't really surrender my life to God at this time. I just basically wanted to be sure I wasn't going to hell. This decision didn't really affect the way I chose to live my life or deal with my pain.

I was in the fourth grade, an average student, but things started gradually going downhill. Through middle school and into ninth grade, it got worse and worse. On the outside, it looked like I was a normal boy–running track, fishing, and doing normal things–like a middle school student would do, but on the inside there was a different story taking place. I chose to deal with my feelings the way my family had–through alcohol. There was alcoholism on both sides of my family. That should have been enough for me to decide not to go down that same path. But my mentality was, "It's all about me." I was full of resentment and was continually plotting ways to get even with people who had hurt me. I held my family at arm's length to avoid getting hurt.

My freshman year in high school, I started drinking heavily, and alcoholism immediately got a grip on me. I was hanging out with a bad crowd and started skipping school. This led to my being sent to Morris Village, a state-run facility. Within three months, they kicked me out. I believed this was a mistake; they had told me another guy was going to have to leave, but instead they kicked me out. This was just one more thing that caused more resentment to build up within me because, deep down, I felt an injustice had been done.

After coming home, I returned to my old friends and started back drinking heavily; I even smoked pot at school. Somehow, I managed to avoid getting caught, but it caught up with me in worse ways later on. When I was sixteen, my mama signed for me to drop out of school because she could not keep up with what I was doing and thought it would be better for me to be out of school than to continue hanging out with the same crowd. I had also started using meth. My mama thought it would be a good idea if I went to live with an aunt and uncle; I agreed that it was worth a try.

My life and body became marked by the consequences of my bad choices. One night I went to a ball game with a cousin. We bought a pint of Crown Royal and decided to leave the game early. Needless to say, we got pretty messed up, which resulted in us being involved in a bad car wreck. Right after the wreck, I decided to move out of my aunt's and move in with a guy they called "the dope man." The dope man sold firewood and crack for a living. I worked every day, but I still did not feel that I had a purpose in life. My daily pattern was to go to work, go home, get high on drugs, and then go to bed. I was letting drugs consume my life. It got really cold one night, so I tried to start a fire, but I could not get it going. I threw a cup of gasoline into the fire, and some got on my jeans. When I threw the match into the kindling it caught me on fire, but I was so messed up on drugs that my blue jeans melted on me before I could get outside to roll on the ground. I suffered second and third degree burns on my legs from this episode. This is when my mother took me back in and nursed me back to health. I was seventeen.

The burns didn't slow me down for long. I was soon back to my old ways, so my mother had to ask me to leave again. Of course, I went right back into the drug scene, but it seemed each time I got a little bit worse. At twenty, I was in a coma for six weeks after a motorcycle wreck that involved alcohol, crack, and other drugs. You can say that your friends can't make you do something, and that is true. They can't, but they sure have a big influence. At one time, I stayed clean for four and a half years. I was really proud of myself until one day a good friend set a beer in my lap with the top already off. He said, "Go ahead. Drink it. Just one won't hurt you." Guess what? That one beer led me into drinking for six more years.

I had five DUIs on my record, and I also spent fifteen months in prison for grand larceny. I went to treatment centers at ages fifteen, seventeen, and twenty, but I was still in bondage to my addictions. The fifteen months in prison resulted from a bad choice that I had made to steal some construction equipment in order to buy drugs. The drugs consumed my thoughts, and everything revolved around using them or wondering how I would get more of them. This type of lifestyle will only lead you to one of two places: in jail or dead.

While I was in prison, I became friends with one of the inmates. His wife came to visit him, and she told me about a friend of hers named Susan. Susan was a very sweet girl, and I wrote her a letter. She wrote me back, and we kept writing each other. I added her to my call list. We talked the rest of the year before I was released. It was time for my discharge, and I thought since I had been reading my Bible, drinking would not be an issue for me. I never told Susan that I had a serious problem with alcohol because I thought I was over my addictions and that it would no longer be an issue. After I got out, I realized it was still a desire. I managed to hide my drinking until after we got married, which was six months later. As soon as Susan found out that I was drinking, I told her that I would cut back, but instead, I drank every day. Time passed, and even though I was saved, I had not fully surrendered control of my life to God.

In early 2009, a neighbor thought I had set him up to be arrested. To retaliate, the neighbor trespassed and came over to my garage where I did drugs. While he was there, he replaced a bag of drugs with boric acid. When I found out, I was furious and formulated a plot to kill my neighbor. I had even sharpened a knife in preparation for the attack. But a still small voice would not leave me alone. I knew this was the Holy Spirit and His strong conviction to forgive my neighbor. Instead of seeking revenge, I knew that I had to forgive. Finally, I went to my neighbor and made things right by telling him that I totally forgave him, and I even felt I was supposed to bless him by taking him toys and coloring books for his son to play with. The conviction to forgive wasn't the only way the Lord was dealing with me. I knew that He also wanted me to give up the drugs. I realized that it was time for me to get some help for my addictions. I entered the Faith Home two weeks later on January 20, 2009. I was thirty-six years old.

One night shortly after entering the program, I stayed awake all night thinking about my past sins. I started praying, and I knew that I needed to change and that I could not do it on my own. As I prayed through the night, I felt strongly that I was going to receive something from God. The next day, I cried all day thanking God for what he had brought me out of and forgiven me for. I shared my heart with someone at the Faith Home, and he agreed to pray for me. I called, and the Lord answered. I had believed in God before, but that day He revealed Himself to me in such a real way! During the lunchtime prayer, I felt an electricity run through my body. I received the baptism of the Holy Spirit and was set free. I was delivered from drugs and alcohol that day! I have never been the same since. Now, every day God gives me a choice, and I choose to be clean.

I am not proud of all the things I have done, but I know that I had to be broken so that I could be made whole. Through God's grace and mercy, He allowed me to come to the end of myself so I could be redeemed. It gives me great pleasure to share how much God loved me and saved me from my own destruction, and the same love that He extended to me is available to everyone.

I completed the program at the Faith Home. While I was there, my wife Susan had been planning to divorce me. She had even been saving up money from time to time with plans to leave me. The fear of leaving with our three children made it a hard decision for her, but she was trying to prepare herself to do it. But every time she would have enough money saved to leave me, something would happen, and she would have to spend it. She should have left me a long time ago, but I am truly grateful to her and to God that she didn't. I am very thankful that she hung in there and kept praying for me. Instead of leaving, she stayed, and the Lord has done a great work in her as well. We attend our church regularly while still frequently attending services at the Faith Home. I am thankful I am able to enjoy my family like every man should, and I am now wholeheartedly devoted to Jesus and my family.

I believe that God did not do all of this for me to keep it to myself, but He wants me to give away what I have been given. Going into the Faith Home was a life-changing experience for me, but I had to want it for myself, and I tell everyone that it helps to stay in the Word daily. My life was changed by the power of God.

My name is Zach...and my story matters.

Tommy's Perspective:

Zach knows where His help comes from, and he is not ashamed to tell it. He knows his recovery comes from Jesus Christ. He quickly tells others that he is where he is today because of what Christ has done for him. He knows that Jesus is the One Who made the change in him. He changed the way he talks as well as the way he lives. Zach is one who doesn't just talk the talk, but he walks the walk. He may still need a sponsor and support groups, but to me this shows a sign of humility. God states in His word that He gives grace to the humble, but He resists the proud (James 4:6). Zach is one of the most humble and grateful people I have ever met. He always goes the extra mile to get others to come and experience the same freedom he has found. Zach has the respect of the others in the group. As he shares, they seem to receive from his message. He brings laughter and the joy of the Lord into our meetings. Zach, I thank you for being a part of what God is doing through The Most Excellent Way. May the Lord continually be your Guide.

The Most Excellent Way is a Christian twelve-step recovery program for those who desire to walk in freedom from the effects of alcohol, drugs, and other life-controlling issues. It is also a support group for their family members. It provides a place for them to share their struggles and triumphs, to hear the Word of God so they can apply the truth to their lives, and to find the prayer and support they need on their journey to recovery. The Most Excellent Way meetings are held on Monday nights at 6:30 in the basement of The Alcoves.

Leave the Miracles to Me....
You Be, and I'll Do

The Secret Place Story

by Lesa Jefferies

*You are my safe and secret place; You will keep
me from trouble; You will put songs of salvation
on the lips of those who are round me. (Selah.)*
Psalm 32:7 BBE

The birth of The Alcoves was no small task, but without a doubt, we all knew that this store needed to be a part of the ministry along with a resale boutique. However, knowing something and getting it accomplished are two totally different things. It takes faith, courage, and diligence to walk out the details, especially when it seems to be an impossible task. At this point, the board was not sure how to implement a resale boutique at The Alcoves although it had been on our hearts for a long time. People had been bringing clothing, shoes, accessories, and household items to the ministry wanting to know if we could use the donated items. This provision had indicated to us that God must have a plan for a resale store (which had been the original purpose for opening The Alcoves). With The Alcoves up and running, we felt it was time to pursue the resale store. We knew that setting it up was going to be hard, especially since most of the staff and board were already overwhelmed with all that went into setting up and overseeing The Alcoves.

Not that we ever doubted this was God's leading, still we all agreed to pray and have a corporate fast before making a decision about when the resale store was to be incorporated into The Alcoves. A corporate fast is when a group of believers come together and agree to give up something they enjoy for a certain amount of days in order to hear more clearly God's direction and leading. The Bible records believers fasting before they made important decisions (Acts 13:3-4;14:23). The fast was set into motion, and everyone began to seek God for an answer to the question, "Do we open a resale store now, or do we wait for a more opportune time?"

The day the fast began, Tammie turned in her Bible to a devotional that stated that someone fasted and prayed for eleven days, and he got his answer on the very day he needed it—the last day. After reading this, she felt led to count the number of days before the board meeting, and it was going to be exactly eleven days. Right away, she thought this probably meant she would not get her answer from the Lord until the very last day, which would be on the eleventh day just as in the devotion. She believed in her heart that she would get her confirmation about the resale boutique. If she opened her Bible, it would fall on a passage that would speak to her about this decision; some people would call this "chance" but not Tammie. This was her way of life–to search God's Word for His answers to her questions. As the days passed, not once did she turn to any scriptures that confirmed the opening of the resale boutique.

At an earlier meeting, the board had toyed with ideas for names for the future resale store. After considering many intriguing names with creative flairs, they all agreed on The Secret Place Resale Boutique. On the eleventh day, just hours before the board meeting, Tammie went on a short break at the beauty shop. Day after day, she had opened her Bible looking for the confirmation, but it never came–not until around five o'clock that evening–just before the board meeting. As she sat there resting, she opened her Bible. The page that fell open said, "I will give you hidden treasures, riches stored in **secret places**, so that you may know that I am the LORD, the God of Israel, who summons you by name" (Isaiah 45:3 NIV). That was all she needed to confirm what we all felt was God's timing.

At the same time, I was also praying and fasting. I already knew that the resale boutique should open. God had already shown me this. I had a different struggle altogether. I was struggling over whether I would obey God's call to return to A Place for Us and be the one to get the resale store up and going. I even caught myself saying to a friend, "Whatever God is speaking to me about doing, I already know that I don't want to do it." Though riddled with questions about why God would want me to take on this task, I yielded to the silent voice.

At the board meeting, everyone agreed that God wanted a resale boutique to be born inside The Alcoves. The only question was, "When?" Everyone agreed that the confirmation would be when the right person for the job stepped forward. And so, there it was...another tug from the Lord. Those little tugs were all too familiar to me. The board continued to talk about God's perfect timing while I sat there frozen in time, now knowing for sure that this was the "something" that God was about to call me to; and I knew that I didn't want to do it. Just thinking about the task made me tired! However, I knew that God would have to speak to my heart and show me exactly what I was supposed to do and how to do it.

On the way home that night, the wheels in my head began to turn. I could already visualize The Secret Place Resale Boutique! I found myself daydreaming a bit about it all and then in the very next second arguing with the Lord. It was only natural for me to like the idea of a store such as this inside The Alcoves. One of my greatest pastimes was frequenting resale stores and finding treasures from someone else's junk. Half of me was "in" it while the other half of me was not! In the middle of this tug of war, I cried out and said, "Ok Lord...this is your hard-headed, strong-willed child asking you for a confirmation. You alone are God, and You know what it will take to melt my heart and convince me to take on this enormous task that seems bigger than me. So if you would, please send me a confirmation."

The next day at church, during the prayer time, I opened my Bible. My eyes fell on Psalm 91, "He who dwells in the *Secret Place* of the Most High shall remain stable and fixed under the shadow of the Almighty" (Psalm 91:1 AMP). The verse went on to say, "A thousand may fall at your side, ten thousand at your right hand, but it shall not come near you. Only a spectator shall you be [yourself inaccessible in the *Secret Place...*]... because you have made the Lord your refuge and the Most High your dwelling place" (Psalm 91:7-8 AMP). To see these words pop out of God's Word for me was so surreal. It was a defining moment for me, but God in all of His gracious mercy was still ready and willing to give me more confirmations of His will. God knew me inside and out, and He knew that I would ask for more than one confirmation.

The next morning I turned to my devotion from *Come Away My Beloved* and began to read:

I will make you a blessing. I will make you as My ambassador, a sweet savor of life and grace. Through your saltiness, others will become thirsty. Through your joy, others will long for reality. Through your peace and confidence, others will seek Me, and they shall find Me. Leave the miracles to Me. You be, and I'll do.[1]

Wow, what an amazing Word from the Lord found in that devotional! God was graciously showing me that I didn't need to be selfish. I needed to share myself with people in God's way. And part of that "way" was starting The Secret Place Boutique. The task at hand would be overwhelming in human strength, but God was just letting me know, "Leave the miracles to Me....You BE, and I will DO."

A week later, again at church, there was another confirmation. Someone stood up during share time to tell about a recent experience. She kept saying that this was something that had happened three weeks ago, but she just felt strongly that today was the day that she needed to share this account. In closing, she read Psalm 91! There it was again....the Secret Place Psalm. I knew beyond a shadow of doubt that it was my time to move out of the boat and jump into the water where God would show me great and mighty things. After arriving home that day, I confided in the Lord, "Lord, it is so amazing the length that You will go to get your sometimes 'hard-headed' children to follow You and Your plan...especially when all You want is to bless us. How important this resale store must be for You to lovingly give me all these confirmations!" After I spoke this out loud, the room grew quiet for a moment....I seemed to hear a soft, gentle voice saying.... "Oh, my daughter, if you only knew....the great plans....if you only knew."

The next day, I called Tammie and told her that I was the one who was to start up The Secret Place Boutique. So I set out planning the next steps to implementing the opening of the store. There were many details to iron out, but I knew that the Lord would take care of the needs. One of our very first needs was fixtures. Most of these had been donated before we opened The Alcoves. We had been given racks, mannequins, and clothing. Just knowing that these were already donated made it manageable to get started up quickly. Having this much on hand was more confirmation that God wanted a resale boutique in The Alcoves. God also brought in the workers needed to get the fixtures up and the dressing rooms built. Patrick, a seminary student from Erskine College, came to lend a helping hand. He had learned about the ministry a couple of years back when his class had invited A Place for Us there to speak about the ministry. He kept in touch with the ministry, and when he learned of our need for manual labor, he gladly volunteered. And of course, my husband and Tammie's husband were also available to offer their carpentry skills. In addition, God sent many others to add special touches to the boutique.

One night, Tammie was awakened at 3 a.m., praying for a water fountain for the center entrance to The Secret Place, which was going to have a garden theme. That same week, a new vendor who planned to carry various forms of garden fountains, joined The Alcoves. When asked if he would place a fountain in The Secret Place, he willingly offered one for us to use under the gazebo, which adorned the entrance to The Secret Place. Debbie, a supporter of APFU, heard of our hopes to find white columns for constructing our gazebo, so she gladly donated white columns that she had at her home. Later on, another new vendor added greenery and floral arrangements to The Secret Place to make it a beautiful and peaceful place to shop. Patricia, another vendor, also added her artistic flair to the support columns by wrapping them with white tulle and clear lights. It was simply amazing how the Lord kept His promise regarding the devotional that He led me to that day a few months back: "Leave the miracles to me....You BE, and I will Do," and that is exactly what He did!

While the construction was going on, we began to see that we were in dire need of clothes hangers. I felt that all the hangers needed to be identical to add boutique quality to the store. However, we knew that resources to purchase any hangers simply were not available. We had to either use the mismatched donated hangers that we had or trust God to provide them if He wanted something different. Again....God said, "You BE, and I will DO."

Shortly after deciding to settle or wait for God to provide, Tammie had a speaking engagement in which she shared about A Place for Us. At the end of the talk, she told a little bit about the The Alcoves but didn't mention The Secret Place because it was still incomplete. Afterwards, a lady kept standing around waiting for everyone to leave so that she could speak with Tammie. She approached Tammie and said, "I know that you probably think I am crazy, but I kept thinking the entire time you were speaking that I was supposed to offer you hangers from our store that we discard. Does your ministry have a need for hangers?" Tammie couldn't believe it. She told the lady about our need for hangers at The Secret Place. Tammie could hardly wait to call me that night to let me know that a local store manager "happened" to be at the church where she was speaking and came up afterwards to offer hangers! We both were thrilled—over those simple hangers and over the God of the universe being concerned with the smallest of details for this resale store.

The Secret Place opened that summer, just eight months after The Alcoves had opened for business. The success of The Alcoves and The Secret Place go hand in hand. Early on, it was The Secret Place that helped sustain The Alcoves until it became more established. Now all Secret Place proceeds pour back into A Place for Us Ministries, and The Alcoves is self-sustaining. If the board had not been obedient, The Alcoves would have struggled more to get on its feet financially. The Alcoves is now able to tithe every month to the ministry. (Since A Place for Us only receives a small percentage from the store, we still rely heavily on donations and contributions from local churches, organizations, and individuals.)

Of course, God used the community to do all this. Through many generous donations of gently used clothing, accessories, and household items, The Secret Place has thrived. Every donation that comes through The Secret Place has a purpose. Some items are kept for residents to help those living on their own to set up housekeeping once they leave our program, some items we use, and some we sell in The Secret Place to further support the ministry. Other donations that we simply cannot use, we forward to other ministries including the Spanish Mission or the Faith Home. Every single item donated always gets used to further God's kingdom.

Not only that but The Secret Place also provides the residents of A Place for Us an opportunity to learn valuable job skills and resume building. The residents have an opportunity to work in The Secret Place by sorting through donations, tagging and pricing items, and dressing the mannequins on the floor. Needless to say, The Secret Place is no longer a "secret" in the community. The ministry of A Place for Us has only begun to see the things that God has in store for The Secret Place.

It is both a joy and a privilege to know
that when God tells you something;
He will hold true to what He says,
You Be, and I'll Do!

All for Love

The Permanent Home Story

Be strong and courageous, and do the work. Don't be afraid
or discouraged, for the LORD God, my God, is with you.
He will not fail you or forsake you.
He will see to it that all the work related to
the Temple of the LORD is finished correctly.
I Chronicles 28:20 NLT

B uilding a permanent home had been a dream up to this point. Many wondered if it would really come true. We had moved out of the temporary home on June 28, 2005. It was time for the next chapter in the story to begin. Our plan was to build the home debt free, but how could we accomplish such a task? We needed $385,000!

Near the beginning of this process, the Lord spoke to me clearly through a devotion in my *Daily Walk Bible*.[1] What He showed me was that building this house was going to take a lot of patience. We were to pray and trust that the answer was coming and then praise Him in advance for it. I remember one of the very first ladies we consulted about the house; she asked me, "How in the world do you plan on building a house?"

My answer was, "I don't. If the Lord doesn't do it, it will not get done. 'Unless the Lord builds the house, we all labor in vain'" (Psalm 127:1 KJV). Another time, I was scheduled to meet with a gentleman about the framing of the house. That morning, the Lord led me to I Chronicles 22:12-19. I highlighted the parts that I felt He was speaking to me for the home:

And may the Lord give you wisdom and understanding;....if you obey... the Lord,... you will be successful. Be strong and coura- geous; fear not; do not be afraid or lose heart! I have worked hard to provide materials for building the temple of the Lord.... You have many skilled stonemasons, carpenters, and craftsman of every kind available to you....Now begin the work, and may the Lord be with you....Now seek the Lord your God with all your heart. Build the sanctuary of the Lord God so that you can... honor the Lord's name (NLT).

This word began to be fulfilled when this gentleman said he would frame the house at a discounted rate. Also, we soon saw how God's hands had worked to provide not only "stonemasons, carpenters, and craftsmen" but also volunteers to help in every other aspect of completing the home, even down to the final deco- rative touches.

Each time I had an appointment with a contractor, God would give me a confirmation. The day I met with the brick mason, Don Her-sherburger, and the commercial contractor, Tommy Brounkowski, the Lord had me turn to Jeremiah 33:9: "Then this city will bring Me joy, glory, and honor before all the nations of the earth! The people of the world will see the good I do for My people and will tremble with awe" (NLT).

God blessed that meeting, and these men donated their services to help build this home. Also, Tommy, along with several others, spoke at a dinner to help recruit workers who also had a heart for this ministry. From the foundation to the roof, cabinets to the windows and shelving, drywall to the final coat of paint, we had skilled workers in every aspect of the building process who donated their labor and often the materials as well. There were so many hard-working, generous people who worked tirelessly on this house—some coming in after a long workday. God had hand-picked the best of the best who did this work with excellence, many not receiving anything in return for their service or supplies. We were overwhelmed by the show of support and the way that God provided these faithful people.

Grant Funds

We wanted to apply for a matching grant of $150,000, but in order to qualify, we needed the same amount in cash or in donated services and materials. The labor and materials these workers donated to the ministry provided that amount. All we needed now was $58,000 in cash resources to make up the additional funds needed over the $300,000. Our annual fundraising dinner had raised $50,000; however, we were still short $8,000. Time was running out. We had a deadline to turn in the paperwork for the grant, and we not only had to show that we had the $150,000 in in-kind contributions, but we also had to prove that we had the $58,000 it would take to see the project to completion; otherwise the grant would not be approved. We needed $8,000 right away, and we didn't know how we could get that much money in such a short period of time. The very day we realized the urgency of this need, the name of one of our donors came to my mind. I knew from experience that this was the Lord prompting me to call this person. I did not want to make this call and tried to put it off, but the thought would not leave me. So I prayed, picked up the phone, and dialed the number. It was very difficult for me to present this need, especially since I never wanted to ask for funds. But when this man answered the phone, he made the conversation very easy. He asked how things were going at the ministry, and I was able to tell him our need and ask him to pray about it. He said, "This morning my wife and I were discussing some extra resources that we have that we want to share with a ministry. We've been asking God to show us who we are to bless." He went on to ask how much we needed, and I told him that we needed $8,000. He let me know that it would be on its way to the ministry that very day. When we received the check, it was a few hundred dollars over the needed amount. We were now able to apply for the matching grant, which was approved.

Rockwork

As we picked out the house plans for the home, the first plan had rockwork on the outside walls. When John Wayne saw it, he said, "What in the world were you thinking? That is the most expensive thing you could pick for the outside of the home!"

I said, "We are not going to buy rock, but God owns all the rock in the world, and if He wants rock on His house He will provide for it."

Donna Brounkowski took the plan and displayed it at her real estate office. As clients sat across from her, they would notice the drawing and admire it. Some would ask about it, and Donna would explain about the house and the purpose for it. One lady listened intently as Donna shared; then she mentioned calling her cousin to tell him about it. Sure enough, a man named Manley Langford, a professional stonemason, stepped up to the plate. He was a gruff-looking man with a long, gray beard, but he was as kind and gentle as a lamb. He told me that many called him the "cave man." (I imagine they called him that because he lived in an underground house that he designed.) I did not have the opportunity to get to know Manley and to learn how he was raised or where he got his giving heart, but he was truly a man with a servant's heart. He volunteered to donate the stones and the labor, free of charge—a job that should have cost us up to $20,000. He even paid for the sand when it was delivered.

We never had to call Manley to ask him to come. Instead, he called us every month to see if the house was at the point where he could come and lay the rock. When the house was ready for his part, Manley came and laid the beautiful rock. He served endless hours in 104-degree weather, never complaining or stressing. He said, "I enjoy laying rock for the Lord better than my paid jobs." This man's amazing generosity impacted so many who came into contact with him. Every time I look at those beautiful rocks, I remember the sweet sacrifice from this brother in Christ.

Opposition from the Thief

My former pastor always said, "If you are doing what the Lord wants you to do, look out! Satan is not going to like it, and he will raise his head somewhere." From the beginning, we had experienced much of this opposition. Here would be another of his failed attempts—this one designed to stop the work on the house. When it got closer to time for the roof to be installed, we noticed that some of our roofing materials were missing. We soon learned that the person who had agreed to do the work had taken some of the tiles without our consent, leaving us without enough tiles to cover the roof. So we contacted our attorney to ask his legal opinion. He said there was nothing we could do that would not involve a long court process. Then he told us to get another bid together for thirty-year architectural shingles, and he would send us a check to pay for the roof. What an amazing God we serve!

Surprise Blessings

In the process of building this house, we discovered that there were hidden costs that we had not budgeted for. One thing that took us by surprise was the extra cost involved in meeting fire codes, which included building a handicap ramp and a back staircase. Then, as always, the Lord worked it out for us. In this case, the truss company had quoted us a figure for the truss system, the floor, and the roof. We were fully prepared to pay them, but when they arrived with the materials, they had changed their minds and did not charge us for anything. Their obedience and generosity freed up the funds we needed to pay the unforeseen costs of the ramp and staircase. Many similar stories could fill the pages of another book. Suffice it to say that God is faithful and has expressed it in so many ways.

Finishing Touches

Once the construction was finished, the home needed some finishing touches. Elisse Sorrow formed a committee and gathered the best of decorators from our community who had the heart to help decorate the home. Heather, a friend of hers, agreed to take on the huge task of picking color pallets of soft greens, blue/green, taupe, and other matching earth tones. She also approved each room as the decorators submitted their ideas. All the volunteer decorators adopted a room and put their whole hearts into it. This was amazing to me because it wasn't something they took lightly. Everything matched and was accessorized to the tee. We regularly tell the residents at the home that God built this beautiful home for them. He knew the things they would be facing, so He prepared a place for them to come and live in a peaceful environment where they could encounter Him and know His love.

Blessing Returns

The Lord promises to return blessings on His people when they give to His work. All this construction on the home was taking place just at the time when the economy was bad, and people did not have a lot of work. But we heard back from many of the businesses that had donated materials or labor that their business had increased dramatically after completing the jobs for A Place for

Us. For example, the couple who adopted the kitchen purchased the ceramic tiles, which totaled just over $2,000. After finishing the project, they added up the receipts to figure up their total and saw that they had gone over their budget. Within a few days, they received a check in the mail for almost the exact amount of money that they had spent! Many other companies who had given time, materials, and labor experienced similar blessings—sweet reminders that you can never out-give God: "Give and it will be given to you. A good measure, pressed down, shaken together and running over, will be poured into your lap" (Luke 6:38 NIV).

Finished Product

By December of 2006, the upper level of the house was complete. The Lord had built this house—all 3,265 square feet, debt-free. We had just enough money left over to pave the driveway, which was a good thing because in order to meet handicap codes, we had to have this done. People in the community came together again to put landscaping around the house. Outdoor furniture was donated for the patio, and someone adopted the front porch and decorated it beautifully as well. Inside and out, this home looked like something out of *Southern Living*.

On December 10, several people joined us as we blessed the house and dedicated it to the Lord. We also prayed over future residents and the house staff that God was already preparing to be sent our way. This He did when He connected us with Miss Kimberly Overcast who became the primary houseparent, working five days a week while three other ladies alternated weekends as relief houseparents. By February of 2007, we were ready to welcome our first girl into A Place for Us Ministries' permanent home.

The Cloak of Love

Kimberly's Story

Above all, keep loving one another earnestly,
since love covers a multitude of sins
1 Peter 4:8 ESV

Kimberly's Perspective:

I n the fall of 2006, I was working in the Atlanta area, running an aquatics program at a local pool for people with special needs. I had been working at the pool for over seven years, and I loved my job and all the people I was blessed to work with. So, when I started sensing the Lord telling me it was time to move on, I did not understand. I wondered, "Why would God want me to leave a job I love where I am able to make a difference in the lives of people with disabilities and in their families' lives as well?" Since the thought of leaving my job did not make sense to me, I dismissed it. God had other ideas though.

God began to show me through many means that it was time for me to get a different job. It was not until February of 2007, that I began looking in earnest. I started running searches on a job website for a publishing job since I had a degree in English. One night, a houseparent job showed up in the search results. Looking back, I see that this was definitely a "God thing," because publishing and being a houseparent do not have anything in common at all. The job posting piqued my interest, and I ended up on a website for houseparents. There were literally hundreds of job postings on the website, and I skimmed through them, more out of curiosity than anything else.

Then I began reading about A Place for Us Ministries, and God started speaking to my heart. I had witnessed firsthand, with someone close to me, some of the difficulties and tragedies that a young woman can face when she gets pregnant before she is married. As I read about A Place for Us, I realized what a difference such a ministry might make in a young woman's life and in the life of her baby. Deep in my heart, I knew then that I would become the housemother at A Place for Us.

However, God wanted to make sure that I knew without a shadow of doubt that He was calling me to this position. Proverbs 3:5-6 says, "Trust in the Lord with all you heart, and lean not on your own understanding; in all your ways acknowledge Him, and He shall direct your paths" (NIV). God began giving me confirmation after confirmation about His plan, clearly directing my paths.

The next day, when I went to work, I got a confirmation from the Lord while talking to the mother of one of my students. This particular mother was a strong Christian and a good friend, but she had been very vocal in her opposition to my leaving and getting a different job. She had been adamant that I was not supposed to leave. However, when I told her about the housemother position at A Place for Us, she immediately said, "That is your new job," and gave me her blessing to leave. That mother eventually became one of my prayer partners while I was serving at A Place for Us Ministries.

The day after that, I was talking to another student's mother, who had also been very vocal about not wanting me to leave. As before, when I told her about A Place for Us, her attitude immediately changed as well. With these confirmations, along with many others, I applied for the job that night via the internet.

This is one part of the story where you know that God was at work and that Satan was trying to mess things up. I got a call the next morning from Tammie Price of A Place for Us Ministries; she was calling to set up a phone interview. It happened to be the week of the local Special Olympics swim meet, which I was coordinating. The meet was scheduled for the following morning, and I would have the rest of the afternoon off; so that was the perfect time for me to schedule the phone interview. Well, things did not work out quite as planned. I worked a twelve-hour day at the pool, then went home and worked until 1:00 AM getting ready for the swim meet. At 2:00 AM, I woke up really sick. I was sick all night and realized that I had picked up one of those twenty-four hour stomach bugs. I knew I still had to go to work, even though I was sick, because I had to be there for the Special Olympics. I somehow made it through the swim meet, despite being so sick. As I was driving home, I began praying about the interview. I prayed, "Lord! What am I going to do? I am throwing up every ten minutes. You cannot have a phone interview when you are throwing up! However, you cannot cancel a phone interview because you are sick. It looks really bad. What am I going to do?" As I kept praying, I decided to go through with the interview and just hope for the best. As it turned out, I did not get sick a single time during the phone interview, even though it lasted for about two hours.

The phone interview went well, and I was invited to go to South Carolina for a live interview. I went the following week. My constant prayer in the days before the interview, and especially on the way there, was that God would be one hundred percent clear about whether or not He wanted me to be the housemother at A Place for Us. After the interview, I was one hundred percent sure that I was supposed to be the housemother, but I continued praying and asking God to show me. I asked God for a certain salary range and that the job would provide for my health insurance costs. When Tammie Price called to offer me the job, I was so sure that I was supposed to accept it, that I accepted it before even asking about salary and benefits. Again, I was trusting God and not leaning on my own understanding. As it turned out, the board had prayed about the salary and had decided on an amount that was at the very top of the range I had requested. They had also decided to give me an additional amount to help cover health insurance costs.

Once I had made my decision, there was still an obstacle. I was leasing an apartment at the time, and because of a concession, it was going to cost over three thousand dollars to break my lease. The apartment complex where I lived was known for not making any exceptions for someone breaking a lease. However, with lots of people praying, I went to talk to the complex manager, who ended up agreeing to waive the concession when she learned what I was going to be doing. That was miraculous in itself, but it still left me having to pay $1,600 to break my lease. But God took care of even that. Some of the parents of my students got together and decided to give me some money to help me move, and the board decided to help me as well, but no one knew exactly how much money I needed. As it turned out, between the parents and the board, I received exactly the amount of money I needed to break my lease.

Looking back at everything the Lord did to confirm His plan, I know that there was a purpose. I knew when God spoke to me that first night while I sat in front of my computer that I was going to be the housemother at A Place for Us. But God knew that being the housemother was going to be far more challenging than I could imagine. During those times of intense spiritual warfare, it helped me to really know, beyond any doubt, that God had called me to A Place for Us Ministries. Even with all the confirmations that the Lord had given me, there were times that I doubted that I was supposed to be there just because things were so difficult.

As the housemother, I saw the lives of many young women changed radically through the power of Jesus Christ. But I was changed as well. My faith in the Lord was deepened in ways I never thought possible. God also used my time at A Place for Us Ministries to help me get rid of some things that were not pleasing to Him and to help me to become more like Jesus. I was blessed not only to see the miraculous hand of God at work in the lives of our residents, but also to experience it for myself.

My name is Kimberly...and my story matters.

Tammie's Perspective:

For A Place for Us, Kimberly was a gift in due season. It takes a special person to love the girls, yet hold them accountable and encourage them to make changes in their lives. It was evident that God had handpicked her to be the first housemother at the new home. Many lives were changed under her shepherding. Even the girls who were resistant realize to this day that Kimberly loved them unconditionally.

While Kimberly was the housemother at A Place for Us, over twenty young women came to live at the home. One particular young woman started having serious health problems about a week after she arrived. Over the course of four weeks, the young woman spent a total of only three nights at the home; the rest were spent in the hospital. It was a very challenging time for everyone, especially since three other girls had their babies during that time. One particular night, the young woman with the serious health problems was at the home. At the time, she was using a walker, and she had gone into preterm labor multiple times along with having some other serious issues. She had decided that she was going to leave the home that night, believing that no one really cared about her and that she would be better off on the street, even though the temperature outside was close to freezing and getting colder. She was standing near the front door with Kimberly, who was trying to convince her to stay. When Kimberly realized that the young woman was determined to leave, she pulled her own coat out of the closet to give to the young woman because she did not have one of her own. The young woman tried to refuse the coat, but Kimberly was insistent and helped her put it on. As Kimberly began to zip up the coat, the young woman began to weep. At that moment, the voice of truth shouted above the lies of the enemy. When Kimberly put her own coat on someone who had just said so many cruel things to her (even though Kimberly had done nothing but show love and grace over the last few weeks), the young woman finally understood. Through Kimberly's act of unconditional love, the young woman was able to accept the unconditional love of Jesus Christ. If that young woman had walked out of the home that night, both she and her baby probably would have died. Instead, the Lord saved their lives physically and saved the life of the young woman for all eternity.

The young woman still faced many trials. Her health problems continued, and she ended up having her baby early. But God was still at work, and even though the baby was born fourteen weeks premature, she did not have as many health problems as had been expected. The young woman named her baby Kimberly.

There was also another purpose for Kimberly at A Place for Us Ministries. When the decision was made to begin writing this book, Kimberly, who had moved on to another ministry after several years at A Place for Us, graciously agreed to help with the writing of this book. Even though it was clear God had a purpose in bringing Kimberly to A Place for Us, no one realized at the time the full extent of that purpose. And that is just another "God story."

Arms Wide Open

The Yarn Story

by Lesa Jefferies

...your Father knows what you need before you ask Him.
Matthew 6:8 NIV

In the fall of 2008, God placed a burden on many of our hearts for other nations and countries. Although it seemed that our hands were full with operating the ministry, it was as if God was shouting to us to stretch out our arms even wider. For the next several weeks and months, we saw Africa in every magazine, on every sign, inside every book that we read, and on every television show. So we knew that God was stirring our hearts for other places in other areas of the world.

In November of 2008, Tammie and I, along with several board members, had the opportunity to travel to Chattanooga, Tennessee, to attend The International Institute of Mentoring. On the way, our conversation focused on Africa, as it often had recently. I told the others about how, as I had been preparing for the trip, I had felt that we would meet someone from Africa at this conference who would form a connection between us and Africa; and, as we spoke, the feeling became stronger. Amazingly, at the beginning of the conference, I spotted a beautiful African woman dressed in her native clothing who was also attending the conference. Her name was Martha. This small-framed, mild-mannered woman was from Malawi. During the event, she was asked by the host to share a little bit about what she was doing in Africa. I excitedly watched and listened to this very humble lady share how God was using her in tremendous ways to impact thousands of people in her country. She described how her ministry worked with orphanages for children as young as four years old who had been the victims of child prostitution. Her words exploded in my heart bringing to life the verse: "Religion that God our Father accepts as pure and faultless is this: to look after orphans and widows in their distress and to keep oneself from being polluted by the world" (James 1:27 NIV).

On our way home from the conference, we all talked about Martha. Each of us had been deeply touched by Martha's work in Africa. We discussed ideas for getting involved with her ministry and decided on a project that would give our residents an opportunity to serve as well. They could knit and crochet blankets that we would send to orphans in Africa. A few months prior to this conference, a volunteer had taught each resident how to either knit or crochet blankets for their babies. With this new hobby, they would be able to experience the blessing of giving of themselves for others less fortunate. But then, there was the question of where we would get yarn and how much it would take to make the blankets. We had always been blessed with provisions from the Lord, but there were many months during this time when we had just enough to cover the expenses of the ministry and nothing extra for anything as "trivial" as yarn.

On Monday morning, after our wonderful weekend away at this conference, I started my work-week as usual. However, I would soon see that this was no ordinary Monday. Around lunchtime, Bonnie asked me if I could step out of my office to speak to a man needing information about donating items to the ministry. There I found a young man who worked across the street at Steifle's Appliances. He said that he had a donation from the Steifle family and wanted to know where to take it. I told him, "Just bring it into The Alcoves, and we will be happy to give you a contribution receipt." The guy stood there for a moment with a puzzled look on his face. Then he said, "I will need to take it around back to your loading dock in the basement if that is okay; it's too heavy to bring in through the front door." This time it was my face that looked puzzled. I wondered if the appliance store was giving us some old appliances or something. I quickly gave him the ok and told him that I would meet him downstairs.

Once I had walked down the stairs and arrived at the basement door, the appliance truck was already lowering a huge refrigerator box full of every color of yarn imaginable! I stood there amazed. Words cannot even begin to describe how I felt when I peered into this box. I felt an enormous closeness to God, and I almost wept at the thought of all those babies in Africa; and here, some thousands of miles away, in the small town of Greenwood, South Carolina, was the answer to their need—hundreds of skeins of yarn in every color imaginable! The guy that delivered this yarn was simply an employee of the appliance store, and I wondered as he left if he really knew what he had just done. He had just delivered the missing piece to the puzzle; he had delivered warmth to a cold little boy or girl on the other side of the world. It simply amazed me to see this precious story unfold before my very eyes.

After receiving such a large quantity of yarn, I emailed Martha to see if the orphanage needed blankets. She quickly replied that blankets were always needed. Many of the children were infected with the AIDS virus, and anemia was common in their small, frail little bodies. For them, temperatures in the fifties would be considered cold, and many homeless children freeze to death each year. After receiving this email, we didn't need another word to get started on this project.

When we told the residents what had happened, they were excited and started to work on blankets to send to Africa. Soon the word reached others in the community, and several ladies' groups would stop by to pick up yarn so that their knitting circles could be a part of this outreach. It seemed that everyone was excited about being a part of the plan to help children in another nation know and realize the love and warmth of Jesus through a knitted blanket. Within weeks, we were receiving blankets that were lovingly crafted for a small child in another place, another world away.

Our relationship continued with Martha. We kept in touch with her and her ministry there in Africa. In 2010, she emailed us about her next direction from the Lord to carry His message into an area that was filled with darkness, voodoo doctors, and witchcraft. Not only that, but it was also going to be an environmentally dangerous trip due to the many poisonous snakes and insects there. This mission was called the Maringue Mission. Her team would need tents to take with them to sleep in on their journey. I presented this need to the board, and the ministry was able to give them enough money to purchase four tents for their trip. Also, LeZanne's was able to supply the $200 it would cost to get their projector repaired so that they could show The *Passion of the Christ*[1] film to thousands of people in the villages, many of whom would soon walk for miles just to come and hear the message of hope through this repaired projector.

We heard back from Martha soon after she had returned from this 36-day mission. By God's grace, Martha's team had shared the gospel with 60,809 out of a population of 75,089. The Lord had shown Himself powerful through greater signs and miracles, and many thousands came to know the Lord. It overwhelmed us to realize that we had played a part in this amazing mission. God had arranged another divine appointment that left us humbled and amazed.

We always wondered how we would find a way to get the beautiful hand-crafted blankets over to Africa. Needless to say, God had all that lined up as well. It would be the summer of 2011, some three years later, when a box full of knitted and crocheted blankets left the ministry, bound for Africa. The blankets were delivered by our friends from Nightlight Adoption Agency, the agency that we use for our residents who choose adoption. Erin was our representative from Nightlight, and she was visiting one of our girls who had chosen adoption and heard about our yarn story. She shared with us that Nightlight was traveling to Africa soon to do some work in one of the agency's orphanages, Tender Hearts Baby's Home, in Uganda. She said she would be happy to see that the blankets got over there for us. Our initial intentions had been that we would one day go there and personally see these children receive the blankets made especially for them from the special yarn that God had given to us. Nevertheless, we realized that, for the time being, this was the way God wanted the blankets to travel.

In The Message Bible, Psalm 115:1-2 reads:

"Not for our sake, GOD, no, not for our sake,
but for Your name's sake, show Your glory.
Do it on account of Your merciful love,
do it on account of Your faithful ways.
Do it so none of the nations can say,
'Where now, oh where is their God?'"

Knitted and crocheted blankets seemed like such a small thing but could have an impact in a nation far away because of one gigantic box of yarn.

Being Found

Anna's Story

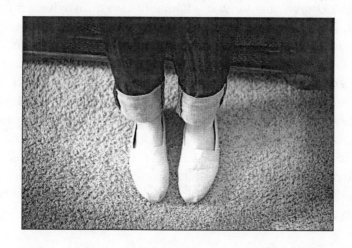

...but let your adorning be the hidden person of the heart with the imperishable beauty of a gentle and quiet spirit, which in God's sight is very precious.
I Peter 3:4 ESV

Getting pregnant on my fifteenth birthday was the last thing that I thought would ever happen to me. I was the fourth of five siblings: two boys and three girls. I didn't really like going to school because I hated all the school work, but I did enjoy being able to hang out with my friends at school. I wasn't much different from most fifteen-year-old girls. Being shy and quiet, I especially enjoyed the attention of one particular guy at school who was very popular. My heart leaped out of my chest when he finally asked me out on a date.

I had never really had any of the "talks" from my parents. It was all hush-hush when it came to talking about intimacy and sex at our home. I didn't have a very stable family environment. Although we attended church regularly, my family life was not what you might expect. My dad would beat me and my older sister, sometimes to the point of bleeding. One time my older sister had to go to the hospital for medical treatment because she was beaten so badly. We never knew why he did this. He was a man filled with anger and rage. He would often refer to me and my sister as sluts. I guess this may have caused me to find the attention of this popular guy at school rather appealing. It wasn't long before he began to pressure me into having sex with him. I felt that it was something that I needed to do to connect with him, and because of his popularity, my emotions would always get carried away when I was with him. So I gave in and gave to him my most precious possession, my virginity.

A test later confirmed my greatest fears, and my fifteen-year-old world came crashing down at my feet. I was pregnant. Morning sickness followed, and I found myself riding to a nearby clinic to get help. I did not know that it was an abortion clinic. I thought I was going to get advice. The woman who spoke with us at the clinic seemed coldhearted, calloused, and mechanical; I was just another face, just another number, just another girl carrying inside of me a so-called "mistake" and wanting to get rid of it. But that was not me. I did not want an abortion; he did. He kept trying to convince me that it was better to just have an abortion. The woman at the clinic told us that it would cost $600 to have the abortion. Since we did not have the money, we left.

I continued to express my wishes of not wanting an abortion, but my boyfriend continued to pursue it as our best option. Every time someone said they would help provide the money, something would get in our way, and I was thankful for the delay. When the money finally became available, we did not have transportation to the clinic. Again, I breathed a sigh of relief for the delay. I knew about God, and even though I did not know God through a deep and meaningful relationship with Him, I knew somehow that all these delays to end this life within me were orchestrated by Him. My boyfriend did not really believe in God, but as nothing was working out in favor of the abortion, he finally agreed that maybe God did not want me to have an abortion.

My parents were still not aware that I was pregnant. I tried to keep it a secret for as long as possible. They were really strict, and I was worried about their reaction. As the morning sickness steadily increased, I could tell that my mother was beginning to realize that something was wrong. My mother called my older sister, who already knew about the pregnancy, and asked her if she knew what was wrong with me. Not wanting to lie to my mother, she told her the truth—that I was pregnant. The news was out; now I waited in fear for their anger.

My parents were very angry, and they were ashamed. They attended a very strict church in our community, and they knew that the entire church would judge them and look down on them because of my promiscuity and pregnancy. This shame led my parents to make the decision to move across the country in an effort to keep my pregnancy a secret from the church and the community. Within a month of finding out about my pregnancy, my parents had packed up all of our belongings and moved us to South Carolina.

When we arrived in South Carolina, I was only halfway along in my pregnancy. My mother told me that I needed to find some place to go or else I would be locked up in the house for the duration of my pregnancy so no one in their new community would know about my shame—or rather, their shame. My sister helped me look online for a place to go, and that is when we came across information about Bethany Christian Services, which is an adoption agency. I was scared when I called them. As soon as they answered, I hung up the phone. Thankfully, the caseworker at Bethany immediately called me back. Through our conversation, I found out about A Place for Us Ministries. Actually, the caseworker had just learned about A Place for Us only the week before my call, and she had visited there for a tour of their facilities. So she was able to tell me a little bit about the ministry. Before we hung up, she gave me the contact information for the ministry office.

On Thursday of that week, I called A Place for Us Ministries and told them a little bit about my situation. The staff member on the other line did a telephone interview with me since I lived out of town, and I was able to move in the following Monday.

The home of A Place for Us was a beautiful place, but living there was very difficult for me at first. It was so different from what I was accustomed to at home with my family, but I ended up being amazed. The house was so nice, and I truly felt that everyone really cared about me and my baby. No one looked down on me, nor did they judge me, which made me feel more at peace living there. They just loved me and gently encouraged me to seek God for the very difficult decisions that I had to make.

Being at A Place for Us was a life-changing experience for me. The encouragement I received from the staff helped me a lot and really made a difference in my life. The staff was always there for me and made me feel like I was someone of worth and value. Through the unconditional love of the staff, I learned that God loved me no matter what I had done or how far I had gone away from Him. I no longer felt like I did when I first came to A Place for Us. I no longer believed the enemy's lie that God was punishing me for having sex before marriage. I learned that God had a plan for my life and for my baby's life. He was teaching me, strengthening me, and making me more like Jesus.

After much prayer, I decided to make an adoption plan and bless another family with my baby. Although my dad had wanted me to have an abortion, my mom strongly approved of my adoption plan.

I soon gave birth to a plump, round-faced little baby boy. I was so amazed at how beautiful he was. As I looked down at his downy soft skin, dark black hair, and ten wrinkly toes, I couldn't help but be amazed at his fully-formed body. His eyes met mine, and my heart became liquid, melting like snow. My entire family came to the hospital to see the baby. They were full of both joy over the miracle of his birth and sadness over what was coming next, the adoption.

I was torn; my emotions were reeling. Realizing that this was going to be a very difficult journey for me, my parents felt compelled to offer to let me come home with the baby and parent him if that was what I wanted to do. They felt that they just could not insist that I choose adoption. That evening Ms. Tammie brought me a book by the hospital called *God's Love for You.*[1] That night, I read it over and over again as I began to weep uncontrollably over my final decision to make an adoption plan for my son. The book helped bring peace to my struggling heart in the midst of this storm. I still have the book and find comfort in the pages even today.

The next day, I made the heart-rending, selfless decision to hand my baby to another woman to raise him, because I knew deep within my fifteen-year-old heart that I could not give him everything he needed to live a healthy and fulfilled life. When the adoptive parents arrived, I knew that I had made the right decision. I knew they would love my little boy and give him a good home. Still, it was the hardest thing I have ever had to do. The adoption agency had tried to prepare me for how I might feel, but there is no way you can ever really be prepared for this. I felt my heart was being ripped from my chest when I handed my son to his new parents and signed the papers that terminated my rights as his mother. When my baby left the room in their arms, my heart went with him.

After I was released from the hospital, I returned to the APFU home to receive some additional healing and love. I spent the first day at Ms. Tammie's house—crying uncontrollably while she comforted and prayed for me. After two days, I returned home with my family and tried to live as if nothing had ever happened. My pregnancy and the birth of my son were to remain a secret. The staff wanted me to stay longer because they wanted to make sure that I had all the love and support I needed during this very difficult time. They understood what I did not know at the time: that on this side of adoption, there is a loss, and you must allow yourself time to grieve and then to heal. Looking back, I wish I had stayed longer at A Place for Us. Even though I thought going home right away would help, it was worse than I had imagined because I didn't feel like my family really understood what I had gone through, and so they were not very supportive. So many days, just living and breathing were a struggle; I was so weighed down by deep sadness and loss.

Because we did an open adoption, I would get pictures and updates from the adoptive parents. When the baby was about six months old, the caseworker from Bethany Christian Services called and arranged to visit me. She informed me that my son had started having seizures, and the prognosis was not good. With this news, my head was spinning, and I could feel my heart ripping to shreds. All the grief and pain rushed back in as I relived every moment of letting go of my son. I tried to remember all the reasons that had made me sure that adoption was the best decision. Helplessness held me in a suffocating vice-grip. There was nothing I could do. I couldn't talk about it with my friends or family because it was all still a secret. A few months later, my son was in the arms of Jesus. Shattered and broken to the core, I ran into the same loving arms that had welcomed my son into heaven. I knew there was no one else who could heal the broken pieces of my heart. He was the only One I could share my pain and hurt with, and only He could get me through this. He did get me through it, and through my loss, I grew closer to Jesus than I have ever been before. Even though my baby died before he was even a year old, I am so thankful that I chose to give him life. I know that it was all a part of God's plan.

It has been almost four years since I came to A Place for Us. I can honestly say that I do not know where I would be if it had not been for A Place for Us Ministries and everything the Lord did in my life while I was at the home. I am sure that I would be on the wrong path if my parents had not insisted that I find a place to go early on in my pregnancy. I received so much wisdom in a quiet and safe place where I was loved and accepted.

Recently I returned for the first time to share my story of God's healing and hope at APFU's yearly fundraising banquet. Although shaking and very nervous, I felt that I walked into the doors of the banquet hall as a new and transformed creation, confident and sure of the Lord's love for me. This was the very first time that I shared my story with others. Of course, my story isn't finished, but this was my defining moment. I began to heal because I was now able to openly share what God had done in my life.

I learned a lot while I was at A Place for Us. I learned job skills and household management skills and other practical things, but most importantly, I learned that I am precious and valuable in the sight of God. I learned that I am loved unconditionally by the One who created me. I learned that God has a plan for me, and it is a good one. I learned that the Word of God is powerful. I learned that my story matters.

My name is Anna...and my story matters.

No More Shackles

Jessie's Story

(Photograph courtesy of Jiri Hodan)

It is for freedom that Christ has set us free. Stand firm, then, and do not let yourselves become burdened by a yoke of slavery.
Galatians 5:1 NIV

Tammie's Perspective:

It's pretty amazing that the three of us who met with her that day had the same initial impression: she had a striking appearance. Restrained by the shackles on her hands, she was not able to move her beautiful, long, black, curly hair from her face and eyes; but she had the most gorgeous smile you could ever hope to see. Dressed in the orange jump suit issued by the state and with shackled hands and feet, this humble, loving young lady captured our hearts. Walking through the corridor on our way to the visitation room, we had felt a spirit of darkness all around us. However, the minute we saw Jessie and that beautiful smile, something just struck a cord deep within us.

We will always remember the day we got the phone call from Jessie's mother. Her tone was one of complete desperation that any mother in her situation would feel. Her daughter was pregnant and in jail, and they would let her go only if she had a safe place to stay. This was our first experience with traveling to a prison to interview a possible resident. After listening to Jessie's story, we saw the effects of a mother loving her daughter to a fault. She had enabled her daughter in many ways which led her down a path towards this prison. We understood, though, that it was hard for this mother to show tough love in dealing with her daughter's addictions when she herself was still struggling with addictions of her own. This sweet, caring lady needed some guidance and inner healing herself. (We later realized that parents in these situations not only need addiction counseling themselves, but they also need education on healthy boundaries in order to help their children.)

We prayed with Jessie and left with a sense of sadness at seeing the effects of alcohol and drugs, which were destroying this beautiful life. We actually knew the minute we met Jessie that we were supposed to help her, but we all agreed to go home and pray about it until the next day. I don't know who was more excited about Jessie being accepted into the program—Jessie or the staff who had met with her. We just knew God had great plans for Jessie, and we wanted to be a part of them. When making a decision like this, the enemy can come in to cause fear to rise up and make you wonder if you are hearing from the Lord. But we knew without a doubt the Lord loved Jessie and would help see her through.

Jessie's Perspective:

This chapter of my story began in a hotel in a terrible section of town where my mother and I lived. We were renting a room there to get out of a distressing, abusive home situation. I was a rebellious young woman and acted really awful to my mother. I was always mad and smoked a lot of marijuana and drank alcohol almost every day. I soon got caught up with the wrong crowd, always partying. One day, one of my so-called friends introduced me to a man named Josh who was also living in the hotel. He was cute, and we got along really well. After a while, he began to spend the night in my room. My mom did not get back to our room until 2 a.m. after working really hard. This made our living situation easy for me and Josh. She never confronted me about this living arrangement, probably because she knew how I would react. My mom worked so hard, and I treated her like dirt. Sometimes when she would try to talk to me about things, I would act like she wasn't worth my time, and I would ignore her.

I had been working with her, but when I met Josh, I quit and left the hotel bill up to my mom. I was really awful to her; I yelled at her and told her I hated her. One day she had had enough; she woke me up and told me that she felt like she was in my way and that she worked too hard to deal with all the partying we were doing. Mom left and paid off the hotel bill. Josh and I decided that since we were seeing each other, he and his cousin would move into my room. Josh sold crack, but I could care less. The only thing that I cared about was drinking alcohol and smoking weed.

There were a lot of crack activities going on around the hotel as well as prostitution and other illegal activities. I met a lot of crack dealers and addicts. Josh had a friend named Bill who sold crack. After I met him, it didn't take long for us to get kicked out of the hotel for excessive traffic in and out of our hotel room. I didn't know at the time that Josh smoked crack until the night before we had to leave the hotel; I only thought he sold it.

That night, we were broke, and Josh had pawned his Play Station 2 for money to buy crack. He bought the crack and told me that he would sell it and make more money off of it. The next morning we had to leave. I asked him about the money, and he told me that he had smoked all the crack. I was upset, but I'd been homeless before and did not worry as much as I should have. Josh, Bill, and I drove out to this old trailer park. There was a spot in the woods where we could park the car so that we would not be seen. We slept there that night. I thought I could trust Josh. Well, the next night, Josh picked up Bill from the hotel. Bill had crack with him, and they started smoking some. They got really sweaty and both started acting weird. I knew that Josh had a gun. I was in the back seat of the car. Bill said that he didn't trust me because I would probably rat them out for smoking crack. Josh said that I couldn't tell on them if I had crack in my system too. At that time, I was really scared. Josh pulled out his gun and held it to my head. Bill put the crack pipe to my mouth; I hit it. My heart started pounding. I felt awful after that. We got out of the car. Josh held the gun to me and watched while Bill raped me on the hood of the car. Then Bill held the gun and watched while Josh raped me. After it was over, Josh told me if I ran or left his sight or said anything to anyone that I would be killed. He also knew where my mother lived, and he said he would kill her first. I knew that he would; that was just how crazy he was. Every night after that, Josh would set the car alarm so that if I opened the car door, he would know. I never dared to try because I knew that he would kill or do horrible things to my mom.

One night Josh picked up Bill. He told Bill that he needed to lick someone, which meant Bill would pull up to a "bar and grill" and wait near the exit. He did, and a girl came out. Josh got out of the car and asked for directions. When he got close enough to her, he pulled out the gun. The girl begged him not to hurt her; she gave him her purse, phone, and car keys. We quickly left and dropped Bill off. The next day we were at a laundry mat sitting in the car right next to a van. Josh pulled out the gun and told me to go look in the van. If there was a purse in the van, I was to grab it. I did what I was told and opened the door to the van. I then got back into the car and told him that I didn't see anything. After we left, we got pulled over by the police and were both taken to the police station.

The judge let him go, but I got locked up. In a way I felt relieved. I was charged with attempted breaking and entering. The first couple of days in jail, I tried my hardest to commit suicide by slitting my wrist with a rusty, dull piece of metal. I attempted this twice and failed. I was really depressed and mad at the world. I was placed in lock-up then, where I got out one hour each day. There were six cells in this lock-up. Soon I noticed that the other girls in lock-up would yell through the doors to each other. There was a girl named ZaDra who was nineteen years old and an older woman named Trixie. They tried to talk to me about God. I was mean to them at first and cussed them. Then one day, someone slipped me a New Testament under my cell door. After a while, I would listen to ZaDra and Trixie. We would sing and talk about the Lord. My wild attitude began to change. I began to read the New Testament I was given. It was like God was shaking me and making me realize my sins. I felt terrible about my actions. My mom, even though I had yelled at her and said hurtful things, was always by my side. I really do appreciate her. I asked for her forgiveness. She and her best friend came to visit me while I was in jail. My mother's friend, Deb, told me that she would get me out when she could find a place for me to go.

One day I was in my cell and was called in to talk to some detectives. They told me that I was being charged with accessory to strong-armed robbery. They told me they needed information about Josh. I told them everything I could remember; I even told them that Bill was with us. After a week or two, Bill and Josh got caught. They both were put in jail on a $100,000.00 bond. Bill got bonded out the next day; Josh had to stay in jail.

I was in jail for a month and a half. I grew closer to the Lord during this time. Soon I found out that I was pregnant. The only thing was—I didn't know if the baby would be black or white. I didn't know who the baby's father was because I got pregnant when I was raped. I told myself, though, that I would love the baby no matter what and that I would keep it. Trixie told me it was a blessing.

One day when I was out for my one-hour rotation, I called my mom, and she told me that there was a place for unwed mothers in a nearby town and that the staff was thinking about interviewing me for a place to stay with them. She said if they agreed to take me, she and Deb would come get me and take me there. I was so excited. I told my mother to go ahead and give me the number to the place. When I made the call, a woman answered. I knew the call couldn't last long because I had to pay to stay on the phone longer. She answered and said, "My name is Tammie Price, and I am with A Place for Us Ministries."

I couldn't hold back the excitement. I told her, "I'm so excited I can't even sit still in my chair!" But before she could get a word in, the phone disconnected us. I called my mom, and she told me that they would have to interview me before they could make a decision about accepting me into their program. She said that they had made an appointment through the jail to come see me Monday or Tuesday. It was a Wednesday when I found out they were coming. I told ZaDra and Trixie what had gone on, and they told me that God was already blessing me. They told me that I would be able to leave jail and not to worry. ZaDra, Trixie, and I would pray every night and sing and talk about the Lord every morning. I think it was Sunday night when the devil tried to attack me. I began to doubt the provision that I felt was coming my way. I told Trixie that A Place for Us would probably not accept me. I started to cry.

Then she raised her voice at me for the first time and said, "Now, Child, you are leaving! God has something way more better than this place planned for you, so shut up!" I quickly changed my attitude. The next day, Monday, I was sitting on the ground by my cell door singing with ZaDra and Trixie. The way my cell was facing, I wasn't able to see who was coming into my pod. All of a sudden, Trixie started hollering and praising the Lord. She said, "Jessie, they are here, and there's three of them!" I quickly started to doubt and thought that "they" were here for someone else. Trixie then said, "No, I know that it is for you! The officer is coming to get you!" Sure enough, the officer quickly got out her keys, unlocked my cell and led me downstairs. I went to this room where there were three women waiting. They introduced themselves as Tammie, Bonnie, and Lesa. They started out in prayer. I knew that I looked awful and probably didn't smell that great either. I had non-scented deodorant and was *not allowed to have a razor for a month-and-a-half. These women didn't seem to care. I told them a little bit about what had happened in my life. They told me about their ministry called A Place for Us Ministries. They also said that I would be able to get my GED and have parenting classes and that I would be attending church. I was so excited! They couldn't tell me right away if they would be accepting me or not. When our meeting was over I went back to my cell. I told Trixie and ZaDra what had happened.*

The next day, I found out that I had been accepted into the program. My mom picked me up and took me to the home, and I stayed there a little over two months. During that time, I found out that I had been acquitted from all charges stemming from the incident that landed me in jail. Mom and I began to mend our relationship, and I moved back in with her and had a beautiful baby boy. I have since completed my GED and am taking other classes to continue my education. God has continued to bless me. I have also found my "Joseph." While I was at APFU, we watched the <u>Nativity Story</u>.[1] A staff member encouraged us to remember Joseph and how he loved and cherished Mary–protecting her and putting her needs above his own. She told us that we need to wait on our Joseph and not to settle.

Tammie's Comments:

Jessie stayed in the program long enough for God to accomplish many things not only in her life, but in our lives as well. Each new resident teaches us something new. It was a blessing to see how Jessie loved the Lord and how she worshiped Him so freely. We will never forget the Sunday when one of our favorite songs was sung during worship. It's a song that celebrates the freedom that is available to us in Christ when we allow Him to break off the chains and the shackles. She joined in with everyone else shaking their hands in the air, symbolizing that the chains had been broken away. Jessie struggled with mental illness, and she was continually in a battle trying to discern the voice of truth versus the voice of the accuser. When the devil was coming against her or someone else in the home, Jessie would open the door and take the broom and sweep him out the door just as she remembered her grandmother doing when she was a child.

Due to emotional issues, Jessie left our program before giving birth, but we know that the Lord worked through her during her short stay with us. This was one of the hardest times when we have had to just let go. Many times, even in ministry, God will say, "Let go, and let Me." We all missed Jessie and thought of her often. At first she tried to stay in touch, but after a couple of years, we stopped hearing from her.

It seems many times when we are needing a little encouragement at the ministry, the Lord will have a previous resident contact us. This happened just as we began to put dates on the calendar for writing this book. Jessie contacted us to let us know how God was still working in her life and how much she appreciated us pouring the Word of God into her and planting truth. To be honest, when Jessie left us, we did not see any way that she would be able to parent her child. The Lord has shown us time and time again that we cannot be the judge on that decision. From this conversation with Jessie, we were encouraged to see that she was successfully parenting her son. What we learned through Jessie's story is that God calls us to plant. We planted the seeds; He will water and bring forth the fruit in His due season. We claim this scripture over Jessie and any residents that had to leave A Place for Us prematurely: "Being confident of this very thing, that He who has begun a good work in (her) will complete it until the day of Jesus Christ" (Philippians 1:6 NKJV).

My name is Jessie...and my story matters.

Hope Given...Hope Found

Candy's Story

And now, Lord, what do I wait for and expect?

My hope and expectation are in You.

Psalm 39:7 The Amplified Bible

Candy's Perspective:

G rowing up, I did not have much hope, and if you had mentioned the word, I would have laughed in your face. Yes, I hoped for many things. I even hoped that I would be able to help myself through my problems. But over and over, I realized that hoping for things just didn't seem to do me any good. Most days I really didn't care what happened to me. I suffered from depression most of my life. I didn't have much of a childhood at all because of abuse. At the age of seven, I was raped by my mother's boyfriend. I was then placed in several different foster homes where the abuse continued. I became depressed and tried to kill myself many times; but when the attempts failed, I believed that God was punishing me. As I got older, I promised myself that I was not going to let anyone else hurt me. After years of abuse like this, you put up a wall, and you become numb to the realities of life.

At the age of fourteen, I ran away and lived on the street for several months before the state realized that I was missing. At that time, they placed me in a home for runaways. My father, a complete stranger to me, got custody of me and took me to his home. I discovered his motives when he came into my room in the middle of the night. When I started to scream, he told me that if I did not do what he wanted, he would make me suffer. So, I ran away.

This pattern continued for several years. I eventually fell in love with a man who told me that he loved me. Even though we were "in love," I was not faithful to him, and at the age of twenty-one, I gave birth to his brother's child. When my boyfriend went to prison, I was unfaithful to him again and had another baby. After he got out of prison, the situation became volatile. He started beating me. We fought constantly and were both cheating on each other. Bad as it was, I was used to it, but now I had children in the middle of it. With all that was going on in our home, we lost custody of the children. Then I had another baby, a girl, but because of my extreme depression, she was immediately put into DSS custody. I know this sounds crazy, but when you are numb, using drugs and caught up in yourself, you don't even realize how it affects your children. There is a blindness that covers reality. But when reality hits years down the road, it is very hard to cope with how your choices affected three innocent children.

Soon my boyfriend and I split up. It didn't take long before I had another boyfriend. The same old vicious cycle continued, and I was pregnant again. We got into a fight, and he kicked me out. So I called his mother, but she didn't want to get involved. I found myself sleeping on the bathroom floor at a local park. I remember thinking as a child that I will never be like my mother who was in one relationship after another. She had eight children, and we lived from shelter to shelter. Now, here I was following right in her shoes. The only person in my life who was stable and could have offered me a place to stay was my grandmother, but because of my erratic behavior and her already full house, she did not want to help me either.

At this point, I had heard about God but was mad at Him. I wondered how He could love me when I didn't love myself. Why did he allow so many bad things to happen to me? The temperature had dropped, and I knew it was not healthy for my baby or me to be out in the cold and living on the streets. I was desperate for help. I found A Place for Us through a HELP hotline when I was five months pregnant. When I called, they told me the only requirement to be a resident in the home was to have a willing heart. I wasn't really open to the "God thing" at this point, but I promised God that if He let my baby live, I would open my heart.

I decided to come to A Place for Us but needed transportation to get there. The staff prayed with me over the phone. They said that if God wanted me to come, He would make a way. I called everywhere I could think of to get somebody to take me there, but no one would. I called APFU again, and they suggested that I call a local church. I started calling churches and found a church that was willing to provide a ride for me. I guess you could say that this was the first time I saw God answer a specific prayer. That was one tiny glimpse of hope for a better future.

When I came to A Place for Us, I really struggled with trust. But even with my trust issues, I knew that I was loved. Many nights I was afraid to sleep because my mind was filled with thoughts of death. The house staff would hug me and pray with me, speaking the truth of God's Word about my past and current struggles. Slowly, God began to tear down the walls I had built around my heart.

A couple of nights a week, after devotions, Ms. Kimberly would ask us to find a promise in the Bible and write it down in our note-books. I usually didn't take it seriously and would just write down the first passage I turned to, without putting a lot of thought or effort into it. One night, when I was really struggling, she asked me to go find my list of promises. She told me that she was seeing a theme develop with the verses I had written down. Then she read four verses from my promise list:

1. And we know that *all things* work together for good to those who love God, to those who are called according to His pur-pose (Romans 8:28 NKJV).
2. Therefore, if anyone is in Christ, he is a new creation; old things have passed away; behold, *all things* have become new (II Corinthians 5:17 NKJV).
3. I can do *all things* through Christ Who strengthens me (Phi-lippians 4:13 NKJV).
4. With God, *all things* are possible (Matthew 19:26 NKJV).

As Ms. Kimberly talked to me about God being the God of "all things" and how His Word applied even to my situation, I was amazed. Even when I was not putting forth any effort, God was working in my life. While living at APFU, I learned that God's Word is true and that He really does love me. Whenever I was worried about my past or future, Ms. Kimberly would gently remind me about my promises that God had given to me through His Son Jesus Christ.

One of the hardest things I had to do was forgive those that had hurt and abused me. I really did not want to. By this time, the Lord had begun to break away the chains in many areas of my life and was opening my blind eyes. One day during devotions, we were talking about forgiving, and I told them that I was not ready. One of the staff turned to a scripture. What I remember it saying to me personally was, "When you are about to appear before a judge, make all things right with those you have unforgiveness towards, because when you forgive, then the judge will grant mercy on you"(Luke 12:58). I decided that day to write the names of the people who had hurt me on a piece of paper. I forgave them and then nailed the paper on a wooden cross to symbolize that I had finally released those people to Jesus. Shortly after that, I found out that I had to appear at a court hearing. When I went, the judge had mercy on me, and I believe it was because I had forgiven those who had hurt me.

Another issue that I had to deal with was that I was struggling over whether to parent or place my baby for adoption. One of the things that kept me confused was the fact that I had lost my chance to parent my other three children, and the chances of me ever getting them back was slim to none. This was my only hope to parent a child of my own, so I decided that I would parent my beautiful baby girl, Hannah. She was my last baby because I knew that I did not need to have any more children, so I opted to have my tubes tied when I had the c-section. This really made me that much more determined to parent.

We went back to the APFU home after Hannah was born. I had more learning to do before I could move out and provide a stable home for me and Hannah. When I did feel ready to start looking for a place of my own, nothing was available. So I started to question my decision. Ms. Tammie always said that God would confirm His plan and that one way He does is to prepare and provide a stable place for the mother and her baby if parenting is His plan for her. For me this didn't happen. I watched weeks and months pass after my baby was born, and still there was not one door that had opened for a place to call home.

Eventually when Hannah became too active to be content sitting in her swing or lying in her playpen during Learning Center hours, the staff at APFU started looking for a shelter that could house both Hannah and me. Everyone, including volunteers, loved Hannah. One in particular, Mrs. Robinson, who helped me with math so that I could pass my GED, was very attached to Hannah. However, my time was up at APFU, and I needed to find a place that would allow me to work and make a living so that I could one day provide a home for us. Hannah and I went to Shepherd's Gate in Greenville, a shelter for mothers with children. One of their requirements was that residents were to find a job within two weeks. It was very difficult for me to get out and look for a job in extreme temperatures of 100 degrees, especially since I had to take Hannah with me. She was so fussy—not just because of the heat but also because she was out of her normal routine. I tried to stay in touch with the staff at APFU, and when I told them how hard it was on Hannah, they asked if I would like to ask Mrs. Robinson to help me with her until I could locate a job. I decided to allow my daughter to live with Mrs. Robinson's family. Looking back, I am so thankful that I made that decision because soon after that, I started using drugs and ended up on the street again. I remember sitting outside in the heat with nothing but my suitcase packed with a few clothes I got from APFU. This was all I had to my name other than a daughter who needed a safe place to live, and thank goodness she wasn't with me. I called Ms. Tammie and said, "God has told me to quit being selfish." I knew what He was trying to tell me, something that I had known for a while but had been in denial. I had finally broken down and knew that I needed to talk to someone about adoption. Ms. Tammie gave me the number to an adoption agency in Mauldin. She also suggested that I contact the Faith Home for women. I knew that the path that I was traveling was the wrong road, so I decided to go to the Faith Home, a Christian alcohol and drug rehabilitation and recovery home.

While at the Faith Home, I really struggled with what to do about my daughter, but one thing I had to be thankful for was the fact that she was in a safe place, and all those friends who were involved in her care made sure they brought her to see me during visitation hours. Some people told me to consider making an adoption plan, while others told me that if I did make an adoption plan, I would regret it. Ms. Tammie told me to seek the Lord and His will and quoted Proverbs 3:5-6: "Trust in the LORD with all your heart, and lean not on your own understanding; in all your ways acknowledge Him, and He shall direct your paths" (NKJV). I knew that when I left Faith Home, I did not want my daughter ending up going from shelter to shelter or being in DSS custody. Many times I didn't feel I deserved any better for myself, but something inside of me had bigger dreams for Hannah. I wanted this cycle broken for her and the future generations to come. As I prayed, I asked God to provide a place of safety for me and my daughter if parenting was the choice I was to make. Then I heard the Lord speak to me. He said, "My child, she was never yours to keep."

Then I said, "Father, Your will be done. Send her parents and bless them."

This is exactly what the Lord did. He sent some wonderful parents to love and care for my precious daughter. They also love me. We talk frequently, and I cherish every picture and visit I get. This family even allowed me to plan Hannah's one-year birthday party. We had it at The Alcoves where all my APFU friends came and shared this joyous day with me. I have no regrets about my decision, and I have peace because I have learned to trust God with all my heart. When people ask me how I could have made the adoption plan, I tell them, "Surrender to the will of God and let Him do the work in your heart. I have no regrets, and my heart is at rest. It is never too late to make the right decision."

It has been three years now, but I still keep in touch with staff members. They are like family to me. I have had a lot to deal with in regards to knowing I abandoned my other three children. I have cried many tears and prayed the Lord would prepare a way for me to visit them just like I am able to do with Hannah. It was hard waiting, but in time, God did work it out. I am now able to attend church with them occasionally. I bought them Christmas gifts and birthday gifts this past year, and I visit them every chance I get.

Looking back now, I would say that the scripture that stands out to me for my story and for Hannah's story is Jeremiah 29:11-13.

"For I know the thoughts and plans that I have for you, says the Lord, thoughts and plans for welfare and peace and not for evil, to give you hope in your final outcome. Then you will call upon Me, and you will come and pray to Me, and I will hear and heed you. Then you will seek Me, inquire for, and require Me [as a vital necessity] and find Me when you search for Me with all your heart" (AMP).

Tammie's Perspective:

This story of hope is really Hannah's story. I remember the night she was born. Thoughts circled my mind, "How is this going to work? Where will they live?" From my point of view, I just did not see how God was going to paint a pretty picture from what seemed like a hopeless situation. This mother was caught in a vicious cycle, and Hannah would be forced to live out the same life her mother had lived. However, no matter how bad the situation looked, I would not tell Candy whether she should parent or place her child for adoption. I just prayed that God would show her what to do.

While at the hospital, I was fighting discouragement. Many times in ministry, when you don't see the fruit when you expect it, you can become tired and weary. And you wonder if what you are doing is having an effect on others. I was at that point after getting discouraging news about a previous resident; but sitting there in Candy's hospital room, I opened my Bible, and God led me to the scripture in Matthew where Jesus said that He leaves the ninety-nine sheep to go after the one lost sheep (Matthew 18:12-14). In that moment, He spoke so clearly to me, "If I call A Place for Us to do this work to save one precious life for my Kingdom and My Glory, it is worth all that is given." Wow! What God was saying was that if Hannah alone was the only life saved, she was worth all the time and resources that were going into this ministry. I wept knowing this was the heart of God that He would send His son for just "one."

The Next Chapter

When residents come into A Place for Us, we always encourage them to pray about their decision to parent or bless another family through an adoption plan. We also encourage them to return to APFU for two weeks regardless of their decision. We feel if they are parenting they will have time for their emotions to settle and for the doctor to check the baby and make sure there are no problems before the new mom starts her new journey. If they are blessing another family through adoption, it gives them time to begin healing both physically, mentally, and emotionally while still in the care of those who have seen God at work through the entire process. Either way it provides additional support through the many challenges they will face.

Hannah and her mother stayed in our home for six months after her birth. We enjoyed six more months of Candy's big bear hugs and her sweet, contagious smile. And we had the added pleasure of watching beautiful Hannah grow. We all noticed that there was something special about her, and our hearts were telling us that God had a special plan for her life. At the very beginning of Hannah's life, the favor of God rested on her, and people were automatically attracted to her like a magnet. Even strangers would stop to admire her. There was just something special about this little girl. She had the most beautiful smile, and she stole everyone's heart.

Looking back, I can see that God was working in so many ways:

1. After all that Candy had been through, she learned to trust again, and she accepted Christ and was baptized.
2. She learned that life is an uphill battle, but what matters is there is always hope waiting on the other side.
3. A cycle was broken for Hannah. She would not have to experience homelessness, abandonment, being a high-school dropout, abuse, and addictions. Candy chose to make that uphill climb easier for this daughter. God allowed Candy to go through a journey that led her back to His original plan, and that was for Hannah to be adopted.
4. Candy chose an open adoption.

Candy was introduced to that beautiful family she had prayed for. God had already prepared the hearts of a brother, a mother, and a father who would love Hannah in a way you cannot describe on paper. The adoptive family has an amazing God story all their own. God blessed this beautiful barren couple with a special gift from above—to love children not of their own flesh or of their own color. When God opens the door to hope it causes a ripple effect that only He can write the details to. Candy now has an extended family that prays for her every day. She has a daughter who will respect her for breaking a cycle and for choosing life although her past and circumstances would seem to give her every reason to consider terminating this precious life.

Many times in life, God uses the smallest, most unexpected things or people to touch our lives and shape us for His glory. Thanks to you, Hannah, God reminded us that He is willing to do it all for just one! It excites us to think of the plans and the purpose that God has in store for you. You must feel like a special young lady to know that God cared enough about you to give you a mother who chose life and now a mother and father who will enable you to fulfill that life and the purpose that was laid out for you since the beginning of time.

A Cry of Hope from a Barren Mother
Katie's Perspective:

It is amazing to me to think back to when I was sixteen and finding out that I had infertility issues. At the time, I did not know that there would one day be a maternity home in South Carolina that would be the answer to one of my heartfelt cries. But God knew; He knew the day I shed my very first tear that He already had the answer to my cry. He knew that a precious little girl named Hannah would one day be born to a young lady at this maternity home. She would be surrounded by people who loved her and prayed for her every day. They would pray for God's perfect will to be done in her life—a life that would one day be my responsibility as her adoptive mother.

I was sixteen years old, which is normally a tough age. Hormones are raging, insecurities are heightened, drama unfolds daily at school, and the list goes on. For me, it was the year doctors told me I had premature ovarian failure and would "never be able to have children." For years, I battled shame and insecurity, believing the lies that no one would love me, that I was less of a woman than the others around me. God broke the chains off of my mind, and I believe one of the gifts He first gave me to redeem my brokenness was a delight in adoption. It filled my heart with joy to see families built by adoption. Then it turned into passion. By my senior year of college, I was eagerly anticipating the day when God would give me my own handpicked son or daughter to mother. The Lord had given me a joy and passion about adoption, but my wounded root remained, and only His Agape love would mend it.

The Lord gave me many more gifts over the next five years. He began redeeming my security and gave me my first taste of His deep love for me. He gave me a husband willing to share my dreams, an extended family encouraging our desires, a church body supporting our hunger, and our first son born from my heart. Those were miraculous years, which laid the foundation for what the Lord would give us next. Twenty-two months after our son came home we were in the process of adoption through DSS. Although we were halfway through the process, we couldn't shake this gut feeling that the Lord was up to something. Sure enough, one morning we got a call from a dear friend from Special Link, who had helped us find our son. She explained to me that the Lord had brought us to mind regarding a seven-month-old little girl. She wanted to know if we would be interested in meeting a birthmother in Abbeville. Jehovah Sneaky was up to something! It was a risky decision, but Chris and I both felt the Lord was in this, so to Abbeville we went. We were excited, but amazingly at peace. Two weeks later, we brought Hannah Belle home after a beautiful celebration of love, sacrifice, and new beginnings.

The God Who sees (Jehovah Roi) was at work (Genesis 16:13). He sees each of our needs and knows how to tenderly administer His grace and gifts into our lives. The Lord put favor on Hannah Belle from her earliest beginnings and guarded her life with perfection. The meeting in Abbeville was symbolically like putting a stake in the ground. Not just for our family, but for the birthmother, for A Place for Us, and for many families involved. He claimed the territory like a Warrior King who goes first into battle. The Lord continually proved himself, reminding any bystanders that He means business in the redeeming and renewing of lives.

As an adoptive family, we are deeply blessed. Through our children and the miracle of adoption, God has healed my broken heart and pulled up the wounded root. We are the recipients of the ultimate gift of life. Birthmothers are heroes. They have given us the most precious gifts, and I believe the Lord esteems them for their sacrifice of love, which He truly understands. Those who give their time and hearts to see the girls of A Place for Us renewed are warriors, and I believe the Lord is delighted. Our family is forever changed because of A Place for Us. What a gift to say we were able to take part in that beautiful ministry!

Hope was given, and Hope was found

My name is Candy...and my story matters.

We are Katie, Chris, Zeke, and Hannah Belle...and our story matters.

A Silent Love Story

Faith's Story

The LORD your God is in your midst,
a mighty One who will save;
He will rejoice over you with gladness;
He will quiet you by His love;
He will exult over you with loud singing.
Zephaniah 3:17 ESV

Tammie's Perspective:

I will never forget the day I met Faith. As soon as I saw her, I sensed that there was just something special about her. She was very petite, with beautiful, long brown hair and a sweet smile. She looked to be about a size one, even though she was several months pregnant. She was very shy, and although she was one of five children, seemed to be just a little spoiled by her mother.

When Faith was born, her mom Pam was so exhausted that she sent her to the nursery the first night. This decision may have saved Faith's life because during the night, the nurse noticed that her coloring was a little grayish. She immediately called the doctor. Faith had symptoms of beta-strep. Although the test results were negative, she stayed in intensive care for a week, receiving oxygen and various medications to treat the symptoms. While there, Faith was given a Bible, a blanket, and a doll. These became her treasured possessions that she sleeps with to this day.

Unlike many of our residents, Faith grew up in a home with both of her parents and attended church every Sunday and Wednesday. She also participated in several children's activities there. She had a rather normal life, with lots of friends. Like most little girls, she had sleepovers at her house or at a friend's house. For three years during elementary school, she had a long-standing "crush" on one of the most popular boys in her class, and the feeling was mutual. Since they were too young to date, it was like a "silent love story." In those earlier years, sleepovers and crushes were the extent of her "girly-ness." She preferred playing softball to playing with dolls. She didn't like "pink and frilly" until she became a teenager, and then it was hot pink (which was in-style).

Rather quiet in groups, Faith didn't seek attention and would think about what she said before speaking. She always made good grades, making the honor roll every year. She played softball for about four years and then later became a cheerleader. Everything was going rather well in Faith's life until, at age fourteen, she had her first seizure. This was also around the time her parents began having marital problems. Faith's dad Mike was in real estate. At this time, the real estate market had slowed down, and finances were very tight. The financial stress along with other issues led her parents to separate in the summer of 2008. Pam and the children stayed in the home, but Mike was not making the payments, so the house went into foreclosure. They had no other option but to move into an apartment. The children resented their dad for the extra burden this was placing on them and their mom. To make ends meet, Pam was forced to add another job to her already heavy workload in the school system. Having two jobs kept her away from home and from her children both day and night.

Towards the beginning of this separation, Pam and her children had stopped going to church because she felt awkward going there while her estranged husband was still attending, especially with all the gossip and curious glances. This is when Faith's mother noticed a change in her behavior. Faith and her sister Lauren, who was closest to her in age, were more like best friends. However, instead of acting like a best friend, Faith became very irritable with Lauren, and they would argue a lot. She would scream about the slightest irritation without giving anyone a chance to explain. She grew secretive and was not acting like the sweet little Faith that her family knew.

When she was a freshman in high school, Faith started seeing a popular guy who was a first string player on the school football team. They were beginning to get serious. This relationship was a problem for her dad because the young man was from a different race. His disapproval put a further strain on their already weak relationship. Pam was a little more open-minded about the relationship. While she did not think inter-racial dating was the best idea because cultural differences may lead to problems later on, she didn't see it being an issue at the moment. As far as she was concerned, he seemed like a very nice young man, so she allowed them to see each other as long as they were at her home under her supervision. However, at home under Mom's watchful eye was not the only place and time these two were together. The truth soon surfaced when a test taken at a friend's house revealed that Faith was pregnant.

Faith knew that her mom was already under too much stress with the finances and working two jobs. She dreaded breaking the news to her. And of course, Pam did not take the news too well.

Already overwhelmed, she knew there was no way she could finan-cially support another child. Pam had always had a personal convic-tion about abortion and had never felt it was a valid option. But now that it was her child in the situation, thoughts would come to her mind, "Would abortion be the easiest way out?" And some days, it seemed to her to be the best option, but the Holy Spirit within Pam would not let her have any peace about it. She came to terms with the fact that, even though this was a bad situation, God does not make mistakes, and He knit this baby fearfully and wonderfully within her daughter's womb (Psalm 139:13-14). Even though Pam had only **thought** of abortion as an option, she still wrestles with guilt over ever considering it for Faith.*

Faith never considered abortion. She felt from the very begin-ning that she was to choose life for her baby. Over the days and weeks ahead, all the decisions they faced began to consume both of them. Pam was struggling with the financial issues. She dis-covered that her insurance would not cover the pregnancy, and she could not take on any more bills. She knew in her heart that somehow there was a solution. For Faith, it became uncomfortable to go to school with all the talk and with her boyfriend trying to deny the fact that this was his baby. So Pam took her out of school and enrolled her in an online school, but this also led to another problem. Faith was prone to having seizures, and Pam did not want her to be alone during the day, especially with her being pregnant.

Faith and her mom had so many decisions to make, but it appeared to Faith that all her boyfriend was worried about were his own plans—plans that did not include her or her baby. What she chose to do did not matter to him as long as it did not interrupt his life. He lived his life as usual: going to school, going to football practice, and then hanging out with his friends. His mother thought Faith was going to have the baby and then make an adoption plan. She did not want her son to have to pay child support because he was a great football player, and he needed to continue his sport and go on to college to play football. She was very adamant that Faith was not going to mess things up for him.

Faith felt very hurt, lonely, and sad, but she knew she wanted to give life to her baby and had a strong conviction that she was to parent her child. However, Pam continued to pursue the best option for Faith and had come to the conclusion that she should choose adoption. When it came down to it, Faith knew she would have to submit to her mother's wishes, because there was no way she could take care of a baby on her own. She was only a sophomore in high school and sixteen years old.

Pam heard about A Place for Us Ministries and called to see what our program involved. In one sense, she felt relief. Yet, the thought of making Faith leave her home at age sixteen felt to Pam like she would be abandoning her child. Her heart was breaking in two with all the hard decisions they had to face. What made it harder was having to decide all these things alone. Alone, she dealt with questions like, "Is it the right thing to send her over a hundred miles away from home?" She loved Faith and was not considering this because she was mad at Faith but because she felt it was the only answer. At APFU, Faith would have someone with her everyday who could care for her and encourage her. She would be able to continue her online classes. She would be taken to doctor appointments and would also be able to get Medicaid to help with the medical expenses. There would not be any pressure put on her about her decision to parent or make an adoption plan. It was Pam's secret hope, however, that if Faith could receive the education we offered, she would see that adoption was the best decision at her age. If Pam could have found a way to take care of all the needs Faith had at that time, she would have done it. But this was the best solution to their present crisis. Pam felt strongly that she had heard from God.

Faith came willingly, and when she first arrived, she agreed that it was the best thing for her. She had been under a lot of stress, and the peaceful environment away from her situation at home would be a good thing. However, homesickness set in very quickly, and the battle in the mind came with it. She began to think her mom had just sent her away because she was mad at her. Many mornings, she would stay in bed crying, and saying she was not going to eat until her mother came for her. Pam chose to do what was very difficult for her; she chose to show tough love. Though it was hard and went against her nature, Pam refused to give in to Faith's request.

She knew that the Lord had directed them to A Place for Us, and she was convinced that she was making the right decision for Faith and the baby.

Faith soon adjusted to being at A Place for Us, and every staff member grew to love and respect her. She was such a smart girl and always participated in all the classes and tried to benefit from all that we offered. While working on her online classes for tenth grade, Faith was able to apply for a community program which was a special opportunity that not all sixteen-year-olds qualify for. She scored so high on the test that it was suggested that she take the Pre-GED test. She did so well on that test that within two weeks she was allowed to take the GED and passed with flying colors. Her certificate arrived in the mail two weeks later. All this happened over a period of four weeks, which was miraculous. Having the equivalent of a high school diploma, she would be all set to start online college courses as soon as she went home.

One funny thing we remember about Faith was an issue she had with our food. To save money, the ministry buys groceries at discount stores, and we rarely purchase brand-name items. Because the girls come to us free of charge, we rely mostly on donations and revenue from The Secret Place to run the home. Therefore, we do have to be very careful how money is spent. One day, when Faith was having a melt down and did not want to eat, she told the staff she was not eating because she was used to Publix meat, and she was not going to eat the off-brand from Wal-Mart. We could not help but laugh, knowing she was sixteen and planning to parent and thought she could only eat Publix meat. But as she began to adjust to the program, she learned to be more willing to eat generic brands and was always appreciative. Pam came almost every weekend and many times brought special treats, always bringing enough to share with the other residents and the house staff. Not only did we all grow to love Faith, but we grew to love Pam as well. Her thoughtfulness and kind words were a blessing to us all.

Even though Faith was the one who entered the program, Pam will testify that her life was greatly impacted as well. The day that Pam sensed the strong conviction that APFU was the best thing for Faith, she had no idea that God was also going to do a work in her own life. She even drove over one hundred miles to come to some of the Monday night prayer meetings held at The Alcoves. God began to speak to her like never before and to direct her every step along the way. Pam also started tithing again, and the Lord slowly turned her finances around. God opened many doors of opportunity for both Faith and Pam throughout these months. Their stories demonstrate the whole picture of how Christ doesn't just work in the lives of the residents, but He creates a ripple effect in which everyone involved can be touched and changed. We always tell each girl, "You may think this happened to you, but God will use your situation to change many lives, not just yours. He sees the big picture when we only see the parts."

Faith's Perspective

Staying at A Place for Us helped me in a lot of ways, but I can truly say that I got closer to the Lord during my stay there. As I got back into church, prayed, and studied God's Word, I grew closer and closer to Him. I learned that although I had messed up and had fallen away from Him, he was still there for me. I saw Him answer my prayers and show me the direction I needed to take that would affect the rest of my life, as well as my daughter's. It was also good for me because I did not have to be around as much stress, and it was better that I did not have to be around the birthfather who had been creating more stress in my life. I knew it affected the baby when I got stressed.

When I first realized I was pregnant, I knew in my heart that I would parent my child, and as I kept praying about it, the Lord kept giving me confirmations. I also prayed that he would confirm it to my mom, who thought I needed to make an adoption plan, because without her support it would have been impossible.

Some of the confirmations involved my daughter's name. When I first heard the name "Hadley," I fell in love with it, and everywhere I went, I kept hearing and seeing that name. Also, I had a hard time deciding on her last name. I was not sure if I should give her my last name or her father's. One day while we were shopping at the mall, a woman randomly started telling me a story about her daughter and grandchild. I guess she could tell how young I was and just felt led to start a conversation with me. The amazing thing about it was that I had been praying specifically about this decision, and we were going to be discussing this very thing at my thirty-day evaluation the next day. The lady told me about how her daughter really regretted naming her baby after the father. I knew then I was supposed to give her my last name. I know that conversation did not just happen by chance

Another confirmation was that my mom's finances improved enough that she was able to afford to buy a house, which was much larger than the apartment we had been living in. This would mean me and the baby would have a room all to ourselves. This was a miracle because she had given up one of her jobs so that she could spend more time at home taking care of her children and the house.

Little by little, I saw the Lord showing my mom the plan he had for me and Hadley. By the way, another one of the things He did to help my mom see that parenting was the right decision for me also involved the name Hadley. Not only did I see and hear this name everywhere I went, but so did my mom. She was at a doctor's appointment one day, and right before her eyes on a magazine was the name Hadley. Another day, she called one of the department stores to speak with someone at the Estee Lauder counter. When the girl answered, she said, "This is Hadley. How can I help you?"

Soon I gave birth to the most beautiful baby girl and named her Hadley. As soon as the doctor said it was okay for us to ride, my mom packed our bags, and we hugged all the staff and friends that we had met at APFU. Soon we arrived back home where we were welcomed with open arms by Hadley's aunts and uncles. Although it felt very good to be home with family, it was very hard coming back to all of my so-called "friends." Because I had passed my GED while at A Place for Us, I did not return to high school, and I had to make new friends. This was another hard thing to deal with at my age.

I was hoping my little girl's father would come around and be a part of her life and help me financially. Shortly after we returned home, he came to see Hadley, and I took her to a couple of his football games. Again, he chose not to be around and questioned the *baby being his. I filed for child support, and after he missed several court dates and deadlines, he now has a court order to pay child support. He has a job, and I am receiving a small check every two weeks which helps a little with all the expenses involved with taking care of my beautiful little girl.*

Although this has been a very hard thing to go through, I am very happy, and I have a lot of great support from my mom and grand-parents. All my family and new friends adore her. Also, everyone at my church loves her too. We joined my grandparents' church right when I got home. I recently had her dedicated at this church, and we hardly ever miss a Sunday. I really enjoy going, and I need the love and support I feel from everyone there.

Hadley is very smart for her age. She is already watching educational television shows for children. She loves the songs in these shows and gets so excited when she hears them. She waves "goodbye" and "hello." Just today, she actually said, "Bye-Bye" to two different people. I am totally amazed at her day after day. I focus all my time on her and on my schoolwork. I am currently studying in the radiology field. There is less fighting among my family members. I believe Hadley is the person who keeps everyone sane. A Place for Us helped me be the responsible mother I am today. (Written March 21, 2011)

Pam's Perspective:

As you already know I just did not see any way I could provide for another person, but God has been so good to provide for all of our needs, as well as Hadley's. One of my concerns had been, "How will we afford to feed her?" Well, she has food and formula leftover every month. God provided a house with an extra bedroom, and it is $300 a month less than we had been paying for the apartment.

I am so proud of Faith; she is a wonderful mother. She accepts responsibility for Hadley, and she has been such a great help in our new home. It is hard to believe she is just eighteen years old and has a lot of growing up to do, yet she is being so mature in so many ways. I believe one thing that helped her become a responsible mother was a hard decision I made the day we left APFU. I decided that when she came home with Hadley, I was not going to try to take over and be the mom. I help her, and she asks for help with decisions, but she is in charge of her child.

Since leaving APFU, she has taken two courses at a technical college where she made *A*'s and was named on the Merit List. (The Merit List includes all part-time students who earn 3.75 or higher GPA.) She then went on to a community college, where she has taken six more classes, earning all *A*'s and was on the Dean's List. She had to take two more online classes before she could be accepted into the radiology program at a nearby community college. Faith has learned how to balance being a mom and keeping up her grades as well, and I can see her learning things about the real world. Her desire is to get a good education so that she will be able to acquire a good-paying job because in the future, she hopes to support Hadley on her own. She understands the importance of insurance and all the practical things it takes to be on her own. Most of all, I am thankful she continues to make time for her and Hadley to stay in church and in God's word.

Another thing that has been a blessing in our family is joining my parents' church where everyone there is accepting of Faith and Hadley; no one looks down on them or asks any questions. I am still faithful to tithe, and God has continued to bless me "pressed down, shaken together and running over" (Luke 6:38 NIV) in so many areas of my life. I have needed a car since then, and He has made a way for that too. God has also provided for my three girls to get scholarships and a means to pay for their education. Very rarely do I have to give them money. I am still not able to count on their dad to do his fair share, but I am now counting on my heavenly Father to take care of me and my family. And He has proven to be faithful to do just that.

Faith has been seizure-free for six months and has been able to get her license. Through this whole process, I have learned to always include God in my decisions. I used to think you only prayed if someone needed healing or to ask for forgiveness. I thought a person should be strong and independent. I have learned to ask God to help me in every decision I need to make. I am now God-dependent.

Hadley has truly captured everyone's heart; she is so precious. Although Faith still sometimes wonders why I sent her away, she still talks about the ministry and realizes it was a good thing for the season we were in. She also believes it helped play a part in her taking her parenting role seriously.

Remember how Faith sleeps with her Bible, dolly, and blanket? Hadley began waking up, crying during the night as though she was having bad dreams. So now, she too sleeps with Faith along with her own Bible, dolly, and blanket. Throughout all of this, God continues to answer prayers. Just look at how He provided me with this home. He always comes through, and I know he is taking care of us. I still need prayer for all of my children in hopes that they will stay on the right path.

I will be truly grateful for A Place for Us Ministries for the rest of my life. I know you were a Godsend. Thank you to all the staff and all those who support this ministry.

We are Pam and Faith....and our story matters.

*If you or someone you know has had an abortion, or even considered abortion, you may be suffering from the effects of that decision. There is information and a prayer for healing in the back of this book for you.

The Scent of Water

Grace's Story

In my distress I called upon the LORD,
And cried out to my God;
He heard my voice from His temple,
And my cry entered His ears.
2 Samuel 22:7 NKJV

Mid-summer of 2010, we were burdened by a desperate phone call that Sherri, our program coordinator, had received from her friend Linda. Grace, her fourteen-year-old daughter, had been dabbling in drugs and alcohol, and Linda was beginning to see that she had lost control of the situation. Searching every possible avenue to get help for her daughter, she considered sending Grace away. She called Sherri and asked her if she could offer a name of a ministry that could help. Sherri found a name of a ministry out of town and gave the number to Linda. Linda contacted the ministry and began making the necessary arrangements to send her daughter there. A few days later, Linda contacted the ministry again to see about how the process was going and the timeline of getting her daughter into their program.

Surprisingly, all the doors had been closed to Grace going into their program, and Linda was again at square one. At this point, A Place for Us had not expanded the program beyond meeting the needs of pregnant girls. However, Sherri suggested to Linda that the possibility may come open to allow Grace into A Place for Us. She told Linda that she would submit a proposal to the board which would be meeting the next evening. Linda knew that if her daughter did not receive help soon, she would end up dead. Grace's once healthy body had already begun to melt slowly away, evidence that she preferred drugs over food. She was also becoming more and more interested in an older girl who had befriended her, and Linda was beginning to see that this person was not a positive influence in Grace's life. Instead, she was leading her further away from reality and from healthy relationships. As Grace gave herself to drugs, alcohol, and a lesbian lifestyle, the black and white of the truth that she knew deep in her heart were slowly turning to gray.

That evening the board members had no doubt regarding this decision. They all agreed to expand the ministry to include girls in other crisis situations. This change was not a stretch for A Place for Us because most of the pregnant girls who had come through the program also struggled with similar issues if not the same ones Grace was dealing with. This decision would be a new beginning for Grace and for APFU. We accepted her into our program and prayed that God would show us how to help her through her issues and life-controlling addictions.

Making this decision to open our home to Grace was the easy part; the difficult part was getting her there. Still a child, but already making adult decisions, Grace was not going to come willingly; and her mother knew it well. Linda had Grace's sister secretly pack her belongings in the car while Linda searched for Grace. When she found her, she told her they were going to meet with Sherri at A Place for Us. Her father met them there. This was a very difficult meeting. Grace sat there with a wide-open stare, evidence that she had been using drugs within the last few hours. Her cheek bones were prominent, and her ribs and hip bones showed through her clothing. Grace had always been a beautiful girl growing up—tall and slender, with almond-shaped brown eyes and beautiful, thick brown hair. However, the girl sitting before us now was the hollow shell of a person ravaged by the effects of drugs. How could this happen to such wonderful people? These people were our friends, a part of our church family. We had watched Grace grow from an infant into a young teen, and now our hearts were breaking as this now black-haired, brown-eyed skeleton denied that she needed our help. We had no need to witness her in the act; what we saw before us told the story all too well. This precious, troubled girl needed our help.

This decision was not an easy one for her parents to make. In addition to the separation and the angry rejection they might experience from Grace, they would also possibly face the embarrassment of having their community know that they had to send their daughter to APFU. With the home being local, it would only be a matter of time before people started asking questions. However, for Grace's parents, it was more important to get their daughter the right help. They knew that they could not give her the help that she needed. Giving Grace all the love that they could at home was no longer helping her; it was time now for tough love. Stepping away from that meeting and walking out the door while their daughter screamed, begging them not to leave her, took every ounce of willpower John and Linda had. Grace followed her dad out to the car crying and begging him to let her go home, making promises that she knew deep down in her heart she was not strong enough to keep. We assured them both that this would pass, and they just needed to trust God that they were making the right decision. After what seemed like hours, they pulled away from the building, and Grace was in our care.

While in the program, Grace never seemed rebellious. Even though she had not agreed to the program at first, she slowly began to "come awake" and see what devastation her lifestyle had caused to her mind, body, and spirit. Her weight climbed over the months from a mere eighty-seven pounds to one hundred ten pounds. She smiled more and seemed to want to make the best of the situation. Although Grace was compliant, the girl with whom she had been in a relationship was not. She came onto the property on many occasions and left notes for Grace. She would wait in the woods at night and throw small beads at Grace's window in order to get her to come to the window so that she could see her. Her pursuit was relentless, and the ministry was finally forced to put up no trespassing signs and file a complaint against her. Her persistent chase caused Grace to stay confused. However, as the visits slowly began to become less and less frequent, Grace was finally able to see through the fog. She saw how unstable this relationship was. Grace already knew from her upbringing that this was not right in God's eyes, and so the conviction already inside her heart only made it easier for her to begin to see the lie behind this relationship. In time, she saw that this girl did not have her best interest at heart. She started to see that this girl was acting out of selfish motivation. Grace knew that it had to end.

Grace's Perspective:

I grew up with eight siblings in a good, Christian home. My parents did really well at teaching us about God and the Bible and tried really hard to raise us up right. I knew how to pray and stuff; I just chose not to. Honestly, I didn't want to talk to God at all since He hadn't answered my prayers. Towards the end of July, my parents sent me to this place to get help. I felt like my parents sending me away and everything was God's fault and that He was trying to keep me away from my friends and family. Pretty much I thought that He was punishing me for the mistakes I had made.

Growing up, all of us had our favorite siblings, and mine was one of my older brothers Chris. We had so much in common; he was my best friend. When he was about twelve (and I was eight), he started skateboarding at a local skate park and hanging out with the wrong people. They were much older than him and talked him into doing all sorts of drugs. It all started there. He was hooked. He always talked to me about everything because we were best friends. He kept telling me the things he was doing and how much "fun" it was. It hurt me so bad that I cried myself to sleep every night, begging God to take away his addictions. I was always begging my brother to stop because I loved him and didn't want him to die at a young age. All I ever did was pray for him for a whole year—every morning, every night, when I couldn't sleep, even when I ate. Nothing ever happened, and he got worse. I saw him go through many over-doses, to the point where I didn't know how he lived through them, and it was happening often—too often. So that is when I decided that God wasn't real. I was talking to the walls. Why was I even wasting my breath and wasting my tears? He was an addict, and there was no God there to answer my prayers. I thought, "My brother is a junkie, drug addict, alcoholic, and it's getting worse as the days go by. God IS NOT REAL, Grace." With this thought, I had officially given up on Christianity.

At the age of nine, I started smoking cigarettes and hanging out with people way older than me (my brother's friends). It all went downhill from there. I kept hanging out with these people, smoking cigarettes and later marijuana. I was a BIG pothead by the time I turned eleven. Because of all of the sexual harassment from older guys the last couple of years, and the way they talked to me, I lost all respect for guys and thought of them as filthy, good-for-nothing guys. So I started dating girls. I also started cutting myself everyday because I had so much pain built up inside of me from my brother's addictions, guys who hurt me, and conviction. Not long after that, I started struggling with an eating disorder because of the drugs. Because of my love for Christ before all of this, I knew in the back of my head, that what I was doing wasn't right. But another thought would always pop up and remind me that there isn't a God there. And I would remember how God never answered my prayers for my brother Chris, so I'd go on with my drugs and my lesbian lifestyle. I continued to be a pothead, which eventually led to me popping pills on a daily basis and drinking every week. By age twelve, I was taking up to thirty pills a day, sometimes more than that. When I was thirteen, I met this girl, and I fell madly in love with her. She was eighteen; I was thirteen—NOT a good situation. We became really close, and I realized we had EVERYTHING in common. We were doing drugs on a daily basis together, spending every waking moment together. I would tell my parents I was at my grandma's, but really I was with her all along. She made me happy; I wasn't cutting anymore. I was good with her; well at least I thought I was. She started feeding me all of the drugs I wanted, whenever I wanted them, and I thought that made her even better for me because she gave me what I wanted.

The first couple of weeks after coming to A Place for Us seem like a blur to me. The people there would tell me to pray. I got so tired of people telling me to pray, pray, pray! They told me that God would show me how to change if I just asked and that He would show me how much He loved me; I just had to pay attention and look for Him to show me. I went through the motions of the program trying to appear happy and a changed person, but deep down I was still fighting little demons deep within my Spirit.

One evening during devotions, I had really had enough hearing about how God wanted to speak to me and if I would just listen He would show me something. Eventually I got mad and pulled a Bible off the shelf and said, "Lord if you are trying to show me something, then when I open this Bible, you will show me what I need to read." I opened the Bible and it opened up to Psalm 22. I read it and every little detail had something to do with the situation I was in. It honestly freaked me out, so I closed the Bible and opened it again, and it went to the same exact page! With eyes wide open, I hurriedly slammed the Bible shut. Again, I thought to myself, "Maybe it is just this particular Bible; maybe there is just a crease on the page or something." I tried to think of everything that could have been wrong with that Bible to cause it to open twice to the same page.

I pulled another Bible off the shelf secretly hoping that it wouldn't open to the same page. I was trying too hard to ignore the fact that God was trying to speak to me, like I had been asking Him to do my whole life. I opened the second Bible, and amazingly it opened to the same chapter! I closed it really fast and grabbed yet another Bible, and the same chapter again fell open before my eyes. I finally gave in and realized that God must really want to show me something, so I sat down this time and read it through. I knew for a fact that it was God talking to me.

Over time, I could see that God was trying to speak to me more and more. A few months went by, and I had a difficult appointment to face—one that I had dreaded for a long time. On the way there, a scripture song that I had not sung since I was a small child popped into my head, and I started singing it. The words flowed out of my mouth like a river, and I didn't even know the correct words because I had not heard it in years. I asked Ms. Sherri if I had gotten the words right, and she said I did.

After that, I didn't really think about it again. I got to where I was going and went into the waiting room; I noticed that some people walked in right after we did. My appointment was supposed to be in like two minutes, but the lady I had the appointment with came out of her office and said she had an emergency to take care of, and she took back the couple that had walked in after me. I figured it would be a while before I would be called back, so I grabbed a magazine off the table and sat down. I noticed that there was a Bible opened on the table next to me, and it was opened to Psalm 118. Not thinking too much about it, I sat down and started reading the magazine I had picked up, and after I finished it, I got another one to read. I kept eyeing the Bible sitting next to me on the table. Finally I said, "Lord if you want me to read that, then give me enough time to read this magazine first and then read what You want me to read in that Bible before I get called back." I finished the magazine and kept looking over at that Bible, but stubbornly, I still didn't pick it up. It was like two minutes later that I got called back. I kind of felt bad for not reading it, but I had too much on my mind. However, I just knew that God had wanted me to read something in that chapter because I just couldn't forget about it; it stayed in my mind throughout the day.

Later on that night, I went to church, and my cousin Sam was sitting beside me. I noticed that he had a bookmark lying face down on his Bible, and for some reason, it kept bothering me, so I finally picked it up and looked at it, and it said, "This is the day that the Lord has made." I was like, "Oh my goodness! That is funny that I was just singing that earlier today." I didn't think much about it after that. We went home from church that evening, and I went on to bed. The next morning, I woke up and heard Ms. Sherri on the phone in the other room telling somebody that the Lord had led her to a passage in the Bible found in Psalm 118, and it said, "This is the day the Lord has made; let us rejoice and be glad in it"(Psalm 118:24 NIV). My eyes popped open, and I sat straight up in my bed. I scrambled out into the room where she was and told her how that scripture had kept coming up all day yesterday. I told her about how I had noticed that the Bible was laid open to Psalms 118 but had no idea that that was where the scripture was to the song I had been singing in my head all day. That was another encouragement to me that God did care about me and was trying to talk to me.

However, I was still plagued by the pursuits of the girl that I had been in relationship with before coming to A Place for Us. It seemed as though she and God were in competition for my heart. My mind was so messed up with thoughts about her, and how she really loved me. She was different. She was not like anyone else that I had ever met. She was magnetic and could draw people to herself after only one simple conversation with her. She had a large group of friends that followed her everywhere she went. That same mag-netism had drawn me in and caused me to forget right from wrong and follow her into a relationship. "The thief comes <u>only</u> to steal, kill, and destroy; I have come that they may have life, and have it to the full" came to me over a hundred times while at APFU (John 10:10 NIV). Through speakers, church services, and almost every Bible study we did, this truth hit me right in the face. This verse pretty much described what had happened to me, and God wanted me to see it. Over time my eyes started opening to some things about this "girlfriend" that were not lining up with what I was dis-

covering about God and His love for me and what the true definition of love really was. Slowly the scales were falling off my eyes and my heart, and I knew that she was not a person that God had intended me to have an intimate relationship with.

God woke me up in the middle of the night, and a poem began to flow into my mind. I got up and put the words on paper about my now former girlfriend.

You are my stars,
You are my moon,
You are my clouds and sunshine too.
You are my beginning, my middle, and my end.
You are the air that I breathe, and much more beautiful than the sea.
I love you when you're here.
I love you when you're gone.
I am so afraid that one day you will leave for good and I will be left alone...
My family disowns me because I love you...
But the "love" I fell for is no longer there...
So...
I guess I was wrong...
You were my stars,
You were my moon,
You were my clouds and sunshine too.
You were my beginning, my middle, and my end.
You were the air that I breathed, and much more beautiful than the sea.
I did love you when you were here and when you were gone.
I thought all I had to do was pick up the phone...
But turns out it was all wrong...
I love you as a person because that is one of the things I was called to do,
Love God and love people, that's all and that includes you.
But now the journey has to end, my dear, unfaithful friend.

Our Perspective:

Grace stayed at A Place for Us for the rest of the school year and graduated from the program in June. On her graduation night, the room was filled to overflowing with many people as they came to show their love and support. While she was in our program, we discovered that Grace had an amazing gift to sing. Grace had a strong fear of being in front of people, so she never had wanted to sing in public. But while in the program she became brave enough to sing at our fundraising banquet. Many people there said that they had never heard such a beautiful voice for such a young girl. After much debating and fear that had tried to come back on her, Grace decided to share a song that night at her graduation. Simply put, this was a miracle. To watch her stand up in front of this crowd was showing us that God had been working and was continuing to work inside her heart, casting down her fears and anxieties. In the audience sat her entire family including her brother, Chris. He came to support his sister and to tell her not to give up. We ended the service as we always do with all of our graduates, by washing her feet. Doing this expresses to them that they are honored and loved. Since Grace's parents and grandparents were there, we invited them all to participate in this intimate act of honoring her. As they knelt down at Grace's feet, caressing them with water and praying over her, their tears (and ours) flowed freely.

We know that there were times when Grace didn't really want to be in our program, but she has said that if she had not been there she was certain that she would have died. She also has said that sin is fun for a season and that it could have ended in not only a physical death for her but a spiritual death as well. In closing out the graduation ceremony that evening, we shared a scripture that the Lord put on our heart for Grace:

"For there is hope for a tree, if it is cut down, that it will sprout again, and that its tender shoots will not cease. Though its root may grow old in the earth, and its stump may die in the ground, yet at the scent of water it will bud and bring forth branches like a plant" (Job 14:7-9 NKJV).

The "scent of water" ever so slowly seeped into Grace's mind and heart. God sent His "water" through many people who loved her and shared with her God's truth while she was in the program. Through the healing waters of scripture, her body slowly revived and re-awakened as we began to see a new creation forming. The scales of lies and deceit fell off her eyes and her heart; her eyes even began to take on a more vibrant sparkle. She was awake again! What had been dead and lifeless when we first saw Grace was now alive and flowing freely like a river. A river that had once been clogged by the dead leaves and decay of Satan's evil schemes, now was beginning to trickle water and to become stronger, rushing over the top of the strongholds of an unhealthy relationship, rushing over the top of fears and anxieties, rushing over the top of all the lies that Satan had spoken into this young girl's heart. As the water gained force, the debris was being cleared away, lifted by the truth of God's Word, and the river inside of her was beginning to flow again. Slowly the shallow, pale-skinned girl inhabited by the poison of drugs, who had once sat before us denying that she needed any help, now had become a vibrant, beautiful girl who was alive and flourishing. Grace was given a *scent of water* and now she was finding hope and life again. She had budded, and a new life was forming...at just the scent of water! She now recognized the lies and realized the truth, and she knew that God was real. He loved her, and she knew that her life was worth fighting for!

Grace's Perspective:

Staying at APFU was very hard for me in the beginning. I thought it would never get easier, but it gradually did. All of the encouragement from all of the amazing people there helped me get through it. They were there for me through everything. One of the main things I learned was the true definition of love. It is an amazing, powerful thing—not just one of those middle school "I love him/her" things. It's REAL. And the best love you could ever feel is the love from God—your heavenly Father. He will be there for you, right by your side when no one else will. I know now that He is REAL. I witnessed His love too many times not to know that He's there. He *loves <u>you</u>. Keep your head up. Go to Him when your heart is heavy and you need love. Matthew 11:28-30 says, "Come to Me, all you who are weary and burdened, and I will give you rest. Take My yoke upon you and learn from Me, for I am gentle and humble in heart, and you will find rest for your souls. For My yoke is easy, and My burden is light" (NIV).*

If you have an ugly, shameful past, and you think He won't forgive you, you're wrong. He loves you. He will toss your sins away. Just ask for forgiveness. He is waiting. He will comfort you. I promise. Revelation 21:4 says, "He will wipe every tear from their eyes. There will be no more death or mourning or crying or pain, for the old order of things has passed away" (NIV).

My name is Grace...and my story matters.

Butterflies Tomorrow

The Unexpected Turn

(Photo taken on the porch of A Place for Us)

TO EVERYTHING there is a season, and a time for every
matter or purpose under heaven:
He has made everything beautiful in its time
Ecclesiastes 3:1, 11 The Amplified Bible

Have you ever been traveling along and hit a speed bump that made you think the bottom of your car was going to fall out? Maybe you remember that unexpected curve that left you speechless until you made it around in one piece. I remember a couple of years ago joining some family and friends for an overnight trip to Charlotte, N.C. The next morning we would be flying out to New York for a shopping trip. We woke at 3:00 a.m. on a cold December morning, dressed warmly, and headed to the Charlotte-Douglas Airport where our flight awaited us. We were all piled into my Yukon, so I was the one driving and still half asleep. We were talking and having a good time as we usually do when we are together—no matter what time in the morning it happens to be. I was traveling at a speed of around sixty-five when Barrett said, "Tam, you need to exit here." I didn't give it a second thought. I put my blinker light on and proceeded to exit. The problem was I did not see all the glaring yellow arrows staring me in the face. I began to exit without slowing down because I thought I would just merge into the other lane and continue. All of a sudden, a sharp curve met me head on. Slowing down at this point was out of the question because the first time I pressed my breaks, I thought the car would flip. The car felt like it was riding on two wheels. Each time I would press the brakes, the tires would squeal and the car would wobble. This exit was not your normal exit. It seemed more like a U-turn in the road. All six passengers sat speechless, in fear that we were about to have an awful wreck as cars flew by us on I-485, which was on the other side of this curve. All I could picture was the SUV landing upside down on top of the moving cars next to us. I continued to calmly press the breaks, attempting to slow the SUV down while carefully trying to hold it closely to the curve as a race car driver would do. I had never experienced racing, but I figured it must feel something like I felt at that moment. The only difference was that I was not trying to win a race; I was trying to survive this sharp curve so that we could come out alive. I am sure all the back-seat drivers in my SUV were trying to use their brakes as well, but nothing seemed to be slowing us down. What took just minutes seemed to last forever.

The shock of the curve had caught me by surprise, and I just tried to hold on, silently praying, "Jesus, take control of this wheel." I am certain He did. Eventually the car began to slow down, and we made it around the curve and safely onto Interstate 485. After a deep sigh of relief, a "Thank You, Jesus," and everyone expressing how they had never experienced anything like this before, the laughter finally broke out. Actually, it did take a few minutes to get over the shock of what had just happened and to realize what could have happened. Then the laughter came. We discussed the fact that we did not make it around this curve because of my driving skills. It was obvious the wheel was out of my control. We knew without a doubt that we were safe because of the grace of God and His protection. We had prayed and asked God to cover us all with the precious blood of the Lamb (*Exodus 12:21-36*) and to send a legion of angels to protect us early that morning because of the flight, not knowing we would need it before the plane ever took off.

Maybe you have never had to take a sharp turn like the one I just described, but I would assume not many of you have been traveling along life's roads without experiencing something similar. Along the way, you most likely have experienced sharp turns, sudden bumps, or sudden stops in the road—something that you were not prepared for. Maybe it happened while you were enjoying the ride, or maybe your road was already rough, to the point that you felt you would crash at any minute. You just did not see how it could get any worse. It was more than a speed bump that made you jump and hit the ground a little harder than you expected. The turn that caught you off guard was a little sharper than any you had taken before. Whatever your road, it was an unexpected turn you were never ready for.

On August 2, 2010, around lunch time, a sharp turn bigger than life itself met me head on. There were no yellow arrows, no warning signs at all. On that particular morning, it didn't seem like a summer day at all. In fact, there was a cool fall breeze, and the sky was very clear and blue. John Wayne and I had both woken up early that morning and left for Lowe's at 7 a.m. to get supplies for the yard work to be done at the A Place for Us home. As I watched

John Wayne load the truck with heavy stepping stones, I thought how handsome and strong he looked at age sixty-two. I teased him and asked him, "Why don't you put one stone at a time into the truck since they are so heavy?"

He laughed and said, "Oh, they are not too heavy for me."

I thought to myself, "And that is the reason we both just laughed going through the parking lot with the buggy that we could not push." The two of us together could hardly direct where the buggy was going because it was so heavy. He went right ahead with unloading them two at a time and then moved the truck over to load up pine needles. I sat and watched again as he helped the worker there at Lowe's load the truck.

After the truck was loaded, we talked briefly about the youth group that was coming to meet him at the APFU home. We kissed and said, "I love you," and "I'll see you later." I headed to The Alcoves to meet up with a few others from the same youth group from North Side Baptist Church. This half of the group would be doing a few indoor projects at The Alcoves. John Wayne went on to the home to meet the other half to do various yard projects. It was not unusual for John Wayne and me to do projects together for the ministry. He was always there for every fundraiser, every speaking engagement, every workday at the house, and so much more. He was on speed dial for me, and the house staff called him quite frequently as well. I could go on and on about the many job titles he filled. He was a volunteer for the ministry as well as allowing me to serve and volunteer numerous hours a week.

John Wayne arrived that morning to the home with several things on his to do list. It was not a "honey do list." I had stopped giving those a long time ago. These were things he had noticed that needed repair work at the APFU home. His truck was loaded with stepping stones and pine straw and many tools that he had loaded earlier without me noticing. Ms. Mamie talked and laughed with John Wayne when he first arrived and let him into the house to repair a few things inside before the youth got there.

The youth group arrived ready to get to work. I had asked him to just be the supervisor, but what do you think he did? He was working right alongside these young people. They had just finished cutting some of the shrubs on the side of the house. This side of the house had a bank, so he had moved his truck up the bank and had the tailgate down. He and Zachariah, one of the young men from the youth group, had decided to take a break from their yard work to have a snack and fellowship. Zachariah decided he would return to work and pick up the limbs that were already cut while John Wayne finished his water. As Zachariah gathered the limbs into his arms, he heard a loud thump and quickly turned around to find John Wayne lying face down on the ground. Zachariah quickly turned him over while the others ran for help. Andrea, the house staff who would normally be buying groceries at this time on Mondays, "just happened" to be there, and she called 911. Immediately everyone began praying and caring for John Wayne while trying to locate me.

These urgent calls did not reach me because I had gone back to Lowe's to get some more supplies, and my phone couldn't get a signal inside the building. I later remembered that as I sat at the red light at Lowe's, I had a thought that I should call John Wayne and check on him, which I realize later was the Holy Spirit prompting me. But as we do so many times, I put it off and thought to myself, "I will call him when I come out of Lowe's to see if he would like me to bring him lunch." I thought it would only take me a minute to run into Lowe's since I just needed to pick up one piece of moulding. All the while, Andrea was still trying to reach me, so she finally got in touch with Lesa on her cell phone. I don't know how she knew, but somehow my sister, who "just happened" to be less than a mile away from the home, soon arrived on the scene and tried her best to answer the medical questions for the EMS workers.

I had made my way to the back of Lowe's to pick up the moulding. To my surprise, as I was heading back to the front of the store, I thought I heard them call my name over the intercom. It sounded as if they had said, "Tammie Price, please come to customer service." As soon as I came within sight of customer service, I looked that way, but no one was standing there, so I hesitantly made my way to the checkout line when suddenly, yet calmly, Lesa came up and said, "You need to put that down. We have to go to the house. John Wayne has collapsed." We quickly laid the supplies down and rushed to the car. En route to the house, Lesa received a call from my sister Angie telling her not to bring me to the house but instead to go to the emergency room.

As we raced through the traffic lights toward the hospital, I went through a flood of emotions. I prayed every prayer I knew to pray, and then the next moment I would be upset thinking, "I bet he did not listen to me and act as the supervisor. There is no telling what all he has been doing!" As all these emotions flooded my mind, I would not let myself think the worst. All I could recall was how healthy he had looked just that morning, which seemed only minutes ago. I quickly realized that I needed to call the children and tell them to get to the hospital as soon as possible because their dad had collapsed.

Soon after arriving at the hospital, family, friends, co-workers, board members, and my pastors began to fill the hospital waiting room. It dawned on me that maybe this was more serious than I thought, seeing all these people with puzzled looks on their faces, many with their heads bowed in prayer. I remember waiting anxiously to see the ambulance come by, thinking I would be glad to see if they have the lights on when they arrive. Seven years before, when our son Shannon passed away, the ambulance had the lights off when arriving at the hospital. Later we asked the EMS workers why they did not have on the lights. They said they only have the lights on when the person is still alive. Needless to say, on August 2, when I saw those lights flashing on his ambulance, I breathed a sigh of relief. Up until this time, I wasn't sure what to think; it felt more like a dream than reality. We waited patiently as I talked with friends and family about what had transpired all day up until Lesa came to get me at Lowe's. I'm not sure how much time had passed. It seemed really long, but probably less than an hour. Valerie, my daughter-in-law who worked at the hospital, received the call and was able to go on break. She came through the emergency room to check on John Wayne thinking they may let her see him. In the meantime, the nurse came out to find out who I would like to go in with me to talk with the doctors. As Valerie made her way out to the lobby, the family and I were on our way from the lobby into the emergency room. As soon as I saw her face, I knew that John Wayne was gone.

The morning of August 2, 2010, John Wayne and I could not have planned a more perfect day from the time we got up and headed out to do the Lord's work. We were enjoying the journey, and I was most definitely not prepared for the sharp curve that was just ahead on my road! There were no yellow arrows or warning signs along the way. This one hit me like a head-on collision. There was no way to hold onto the steering wheel. The only thing I could hold on to was Jesus and the promises that are in His Word. The Lord himself would have to get me around this one for sure, and instead of me taking a trip to New York, John Wayne was taking a trip. The Father said, "Come." The angels in heaven were rejoicing as our loving Father came to take one of His children home. John Wayne entered the presence of the King of kings and the Lord of lords. What an amazing thing to think about—John Wayne was no longer a retired railroad man and maintenance man for A Place for Us Ministries! Instead, he was now experiencing for the first time being in the Father's house and enjoying his inheritance. Jesus said, "Let not your hearts be troubled; you believe in God, believe also in Me. In My Father's house are many mansions; if it were not so, I would have told you. I go to prepare a place for you. And if I go and prepare a place for you, I will come again and receive you to Myself; that where I am, there you may be also"(John 14:1-3 KJV).

The turn in this road was sharp, and it was unexpected, filled with sudden loneliness and difficult decisions that I wasn't ready to make. If I could paint you a picture of the events that followed, I would be lying if I told you there was no anger, but I have to honestly say it did not last very long—probably just for a few minutes and very few times. I was mad, and I questioned God. I sat in that emergency room and told God, "I wasn't ready for this!" "I can't do this!" and "Why did this have to happen now?" The pain of loss was so deep that it felt like my heart was torn and broken in two. Like the SUV that wobbled as it went around that sharp curve, my whole being seemed to shudder with the depths of pain that was expressed every time I cried. I had never felt this kind of brokenness before; this was half of me gone. But as my heavenly Father so lovingly does, He comforted me and quieted me in my innermost being.

My loving children and grandchildren surrounded me, along with all our family and friends, and in the days ahead, I found out just how much we were loved. Flowers, food, memorials, cards, prayers, paper products, more food, and condolences of every kind came in day after day.

I was going through the motions but feeling motionless. As I looked outside through the windows, all I could see was a fog that covered my vision. I could not see clearly or think clearly. Of all the scriptures that I had learned and memorized–I could not recall any of them. All I could recite was "When I am weak, He is strong" (Isaiah 40:29, II Corinthians 12:10) and "The joy of the Lord *has got to be* my strength" (Nehemiah 8:10). These were the only two verses that would even halfway come to mind for me during the first few days. (Although scripture would not come to mind, one interesting thing that did keep coming to mind was a song from a musical about a poor orphan girl. In the song, this orphan confidently sang of her hopes for a better, happier tomorrow. What was interesting about this particular song was that Kristi had loved to sing it as a little girl, and John Wayne would always tell her, "Sing it again, Kristi!" I truly believe the Lord gave me this song in my heart to comfort me, and I will always treasure it. It is amazing what the Lord will use to comfort you at your weakest moments in life!)

Decisions had to be made, but they would not come easily. Steve, the funeral home director, came and wanted to plan the service. One of the questions I remember him asking me was, "What is John Wayne's favorite scripture? We need one for the program." I could not think of one. Then he said, "I know. Wasn't it the one the two of you learned on the boat at Santee–Isaiah 61?" I was blown away that John Wayne, the one who rarely talked about the Word but tried to live it every day, had shared this story with Steve and also that Steve remembered it! Next we needed a song, but not one single song would come to mind when he asked. I knew the Lord would wake me up in the middle of the night and give me one. He did just that; it was a song which talks about God being with us through the storms we face and us praising Him even though we are going through such a difficult time. I was not too familiar with this song, but I sat straight up in the bed at three a.m. singing it.

Although I could see God's hand in the very details of that day, and I knew this early morning song was from God, I still had questions that needed to be answered. I asked the Lord if somehow He could show me why the time was now. Why so soon? Why so quickly? He tells us if we ask, He will answer, and sure enough, as I made my way into my office that morning, I looked down to find a book that Amber, my daughter-in-law, had just returned. It was *The Power of a Praying Wife*, by Stormie Omartian. I felt led to open it up to see what God would turn me to. I turned right to the prayer I had prayed many times for John Wayne. I even had it marked with his name on it. It was the one about "His Health." The part that I had underlined went something like this: "Oh LORD my God, I pray my husband will live a healthy life, and when death does come, may it be accompanied by peace and not unbearable suffering and agony. Thank You, Lord, You will be there to welcome him into Your presence and not a moment before Your appointed hour."[1] These things comforted me, and there was no way I could deny that this was part of God's plan and that He had not left me, and He had not forsaken John Wayne. These truths would help me to be prepared for the next day we would face, the actual funeral service and burial.

It was time for others to come and share in our grief. The visitation line wrapped around the church as person after person came to express their condolences. Steve said over nine hundred people came through the line. Each person had a kind hug, smile, or encouraging word. But I will never forget the current girls at the home along with some of the previous girls from A Place for Us that came through that line; they were crying as if we were a part of their very own family. These girls hold a special place in my heart, and these are memories I will never forget!

Eventually it was time to return to work, and things had to somehow get back to normal. However, the acts of kindness did not end for weeks and months, and many are still going on to this day. For weeks, there would be dozens of cards, and each one would say just what I needed for that day. I remember the hand-written words in one particular card which expressed perfectly the way I was feeling: "I know that you are probably not even able to pray for yourself right now, but rest in God's peace, knowing that the Holy Spirit is interceding on your behalf, and He knows your every weakness and your every need." The day I returned to the beauty shop, I was working and trying to see through the fog that had incased my eyes and would not lift. I was going through the motions and trying to take care of my clients' needs when I got a surprise visit from a dear partner of the ministry who had previously lost her husband to a massive heart attack. She brought a book that she wanted to give to me entitled *Grace for the Widow: A Journey Through the Fog of Loss*. I thought, "This describes my emotions exactly." I shared with her that I had been feeling this way and had wondered what was going on. She told me that she had felt the same way, and it had lasted about six months. She encouraged me to read the book, which I did, and it helped me immensely as I dealt with all sorts of thoughts and feelings.

Day by day, as I sought the Lord to be the "lifter of my head" (Psalm 3:3 ESV), He gently and carefully comforted my spirit. Condolences continued to come from many in the community through various gifts. Memorials poured in to the ministry, and one day I shared with my mother that the total was around $4,000. She said, "Tammie, I would not be surprised if the memorials for John Wayne reach $10,000." I thought to myself, "There is no way." In the past, we have had many people request that memorials be made to A Place for Us, but we have never had that kind of money come in. Just days after that conversation, Lesa called to tell me that we were only $300 short of the $10,000 mark. We did not share this with anyone else. Soon, Edie Brock, one of my co-workers, came into The Alcoves and said that she would like to make a donation as a memorial to John Wayne. It was a check for $300!

Daily I experienced God stories and blessings, whether it was through our children, grandchildren, a customer, through God's Word, or through a butterfly. The butterfly is a sign of resurrection and new life. They normally come out in March and April. But when John Wayne passed away, the very next day a butterfly appeared on the porch at the home of A Place for Us; it stayed around the house for three days. From there we began to see at least fifty to one hundred butterflies a day! I will never forget when Faith, one of the residents, came to see me a couple of days after John Wayne's passing. She asked if I had noticed all the butterflies. I told her that I had not. She went on to share that ever since the day John Wayne went to be with Jesus, there had been butterflies everywhere. She knew this was from God, and it brought her comfort and confirmed to her that everything was going to be all right. The Lord has continued to send me butterflies as a confirmation that He is in control and will guide me along the way.

Butterflies have a message for everyone no matter what you are going through. We often use them as an illustration for the residents in our program at APFU. Many times in life, it feels as though we are in a dark place where we feel bound and there does not seem like a way out. However, as we push and allow the Lord's transformation to take place in our lives, we are able to come out and fly. While we are wrapped up inside that cocoon, it seems lonely and dark, and the way seems hopeless; but we have to push our way through the haze by choosing to believe what God's Word says and decreeing and declaring it over our lives day by day—even when it is hard, and we don't want to say it or believe it. This helps get that peace back... that "peace that passes all understanding" (Philippians 4:7 AKJV). It may be as simple as saying, "When I am weak, He is strong" (Isaiah 40:29, II Corinthians 12:10). We must hold on to the truth because it is the truth that sets us free (John 8:32)! He makes everything beautiful in His time (Ecclesiastes 3:11). Many days, I would question the Lord. I wondered how I could pay my bills working two days a week at the beauty shop or how I would be able to take care of my home and my yard. How would I live with the loneliness and all the other things that confronted me every day? On one of these days, I turned to Psalm 119:25-33 in the Message Bible:

I'm feeling terrible—I couldn't feel worse!
Get me on my feet again. You promised, remember?
When I told my story, You responded;
train me well in Your deep wisdom.
Help me understand these things inside
and out so I can ponder Your miracle-wonders.

My sad life's dilapidated, a falling-down barn;
build me up again by Your Word.
Barricade the road that goes Nowhere;
grace me with Your clear revelation.
I choose the true road to Somewhere,
I post Your road signs at every curve and corner.
I grasp and cling to whatever You tell me;
God, don't let me down!
I'll run the course You lay out for me….
if You'll just show me how.
God, teach me lessons for living
so I can stay the course.

This passage brought me such comfort and peace. The Lord used many other scriptures to speak His comfort to me as well:

Jesus said,"I am the resurrection and the life. He who believes in Me, though he may die, he shall live. And whoever lives and believes in Me shall never die" (John 11:25-26 NKJV).

Peace I leave with you, My peace I give to you; not as the world gives do I give to you. Let not your heart be troubled, neither let it be afraid (John 14:27 ESV).

Call to Me, and I will answer you, and show you great and mighty things, which you do not know (Jeremiah 33:3 NKJV).

I weep with grief; encourage me by Your Word (Psalm 119:28 NLT).

Weeping may endure for a night, but joy comes in the morning (Psalm 30:5 NKJV).

…to comfort all who mourn, and provide for those who grieve in Zion, to bestow on them a crown of beauty instead of ashes, the oil of joy instead of mourning, and a garment of praise instead of…despair (Isaiah 61:2b-3a NIV).

Good people pass away; the godly often die before their time. But no one seems to care or wonder why. No one seems to understand that God is protecting them from the evil to come. For those who follow Godly paths will rest in peace when they die (Isaiah 57:1-2 NLT).

God's Word is like a treasure chest. If we are faithful to God and His Word, we will reap the benefits of that treasure. Unlike a retirement account, which you only get benefits from when you reach retirement age, this treasure pays dividends every day if you let it, and there is no penalty for early distribution. This doesn't mean that we will never experience grief or suffer an unexpected loss. When I lost my daddy in December of 2009, I never expected that I would lose my husband eight months later. But I can say that God was there for me, and He was faithful to comfort and console me. And He will do the same for you. God's promises are what will hold you in the middle of the night, and He will comfort you by His Holy Spirit, because He is the Comforter.

Gradually the fog lifted; still my Lord of hosts is daily helping me to walk through this journey, one step at a time. In weak moments, I may wonder how I will make it, but I know that I will because Isaiah 54:5 says, "For your Maker is your husband, the Lord of hosts is His name; and your Redeemer is the Holy One of Israel; He is called the God of the whole earth" (NKJV). Maybe your loss is different from mine. If you have lost a loved one through death, pain, addiction, divorce, or by placing your baby with adoptive parents, remember, there are some things we never get over; but with Jesus Christ, you will get through them all. No one ever desires to become homeless, an orphan, or a widow, but God's Word mentions over sixty times that you are close to His heart, and when you are weak, He is strong!

The greatest promise we have been given is that Jesus Christ paid for our sins through the shedding of His blood, and because of Him, we have eternal life. Those who are in Christ never see each other for the last time. Instead of saying, "Good-bye" the last time I saw John Wayne, I said, "See you later." Thank You, Jesus, that this is Your promise, and there will be a day that I will see it fulfilled. Until then, I rest in Your peace.

This is the scripture the Lord turned me to at three in the morning to be used for the funeral service:

In Loving Memory of John Wayne Price Sr.

Better things...will come with salvation....For God is not unfair. He will not forget how hard you have worked for Him, and how you have shown love to Him by caring for others, especially Christians. His desire is that we would keep on loving others as long as our life lasts. In order to make certain that what we hope for will come true. Then we will not become spiritually dull and indifferent; instead, you will follow the example of those who are going to inherit God's promises because of their faith and patience (Hebrews 6:9b-12, Re-phrased NLT).

He Is More Than a Story

The Conclusion

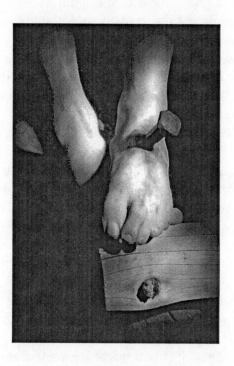

I've preached You to the whole congregation,
I've kept back nothing, GOD—You know that.
I didn't keep the news of Your ways
a secret, didn't keep it to myself.
I told it all, how dependable You are, how thorough.
I didn't hold back pieces of love and truth
for myself alone. I told it all,
let the congregation know the whole story.
Psalm 40:10 The Message Bible

In the beginning, I talked about the funny true story of my mowing grass in a pair of royal blue stilettos and how doing this led me into a whole new chapter in my life. It wasn't my intention that morning to put those shoes on so that I could mow grass in them. It was just a quick notion I had to do something nice for someone I was really fond of. I had no earthly idea that it would be a defining moment, which turned another page in my story. Even so, we start out every day making choices that ultimately lead us somewhere. Of course, we hope they lead us to something good, like the yard work that led to a wonderful marriage, but what about the choices that lead us down the wrong paths? I don't believe there are many people who get up one day and decide to become pregnant out of wedlock, especially when becoming pregnant sometimes leads to other issues like possible homelessness or potential heartache over a decision to have to make an adoption plan or making a choice to terminate a life. I don't believe people decide one day to become an alcoholic or an addict. But, unfortunately, it becomes a way of life for a lot of people because of their choices. Problems like these are not limited to just one certain class of people. They hit all social economic classes. Often it is hard to understand someone else's story unless you have walked in that person's shoes. As we have shared these personal stories of men and women from different paths in life, we hope you have been able to "walk in their shoes" for a moment and connect to at least one of these stories in a personal way. At times, it was difficult to tell the stories of hardship and painful pasts—even my own. But I realized that I just couldn't put the past aside as if it had never happened and write just the good stuff, the "happily ever after" stuff. You see, in order to see the whole picture, you first have to understand someone's past and where that person came from before you can appreciate and see the good stuff of God's grace in his or her life. Jesus is the only One Who can truly write the final *happily ever after*'s of our *once upon a time*'s.

For each resident that comes through the doors of A Place for Us Ministries, we as staff hold on to the promise that His Word does not "return void" (Isaiah 55:11 NKJV). The greatest truth we hope the residents stand on is the truth of who they are in Christ—that "if anyone is in Christ, he is a new creation; old things have passed away; behold, all things have become new" (II Corinthians 5:17 NKJV).

We also pray that God will continue to reveal the truth of His character and His love for them. As one of the residents once put it, "God did not come up with all these rules just to say 'No.' He came up with them so that He could say, 'Yes' to the good things He had stored up for us and to keep us from going through many heartaches that weren't a part of His plan in the first place." When He looks into your face, there is nothing that you can ever do to make Him stop loving you! The great thing is that He loved us when we were still in sin. We don't have to get it all right before He will accept us. He is always there waiting patiently. He is the sweetest Gentleman I have ever known. These stories did not even come close to describing the magnitude and power of His great love for us. Life can be hard, cold, and lonely, but you can always look back and see God's faithfulness. You may have to look a little longer and harder at times, but His faithfulness has been and always will be there.

What About Me?

Many who have read these stories may be wondering how all these "God things" can happen. Maybe you are asking, "Are these 'God stories' even true?" and "Why hasn't anything like this happened for me?" My challenge to you is this. Why not give Him permission? He waits patiently to be invited to come into your world. God doesn't force Himself into our stories; it is only when we look for Him that He will be found. Jesus said, "Ask, and it will be given to you; seek, and you will find; knock, and the door will be opened to you. For everyone who asks receives, and he who seeks finds, and to him who knocks the door will be opened" (Luke 11:9 NIV). We need to have the confidence and faith reflected in Micah's prayer: "As for me, I look to the Lord for His help; I wait confidently for God to save me, and my God will certainly hear me"(Micah 7:7, NLT).

Faith in What We Don't See

Early on in the ministry, it was clear that we had to walk by faith. It took faith to believe in advance through circumstances that would only make sense in reverse. It would also take courage. Can you even imagine the kind of faith and courage it took Noah to build the ark? "By faith, Noah built a ship in the middle of dry land. He was warned about something he couldn't see, and acted on what he was told. The result? His family was saved. His act of faith drew a sharp line between the evil of the unbelieving world and the rightness of the believing world. As a result, Noah became intimate with God" (Hebrews 11:7 MSG). God honored Noah and sent him proof of his hope in the form of an olive leaf. There is hope everyday in your journey when you walk in faith and courage; it is not until we take the first step that our faith becomes real.

When you are facing life's difficult questions—like a call God has placed on your life, trying to make a decision to get help for a life-controlling issue, making a change in your career, going back to school—whatever the decision, you will never get there without faith to believe that you can. Many of the life stories you have read were about people that walked in courage and allowed God and His power to change their lives around. Courage is what helped them take another step toward God and away from the things that held them captive. Pray and ask God to give you the faith of a mustard seed (Luke 17:6) and the obedience to walk it out. You will begin to see your faith grow once again or maybe for the very first time. You will hear His voice and know which way to go. You will have the hope you need in order to praise Him through the storm. You will also know when your faith requires the courage to be still and know that He is God (Psalm 46:10).

After reading this book, I hope you realize that you too have a story that can be used to change another person's life. God wants to do a new thing. Don't keep your eyes on the past, but press forward to what lies ahead and know that He can remove any obstacle. You are a child of the King, The Most High God, and your story matters. You may laugh after reading that last sentence thinking that your story has never been anything but a mess. But Jesus takes our *messes* and turns them into a *message* for His glory. Jesus went to great measures to purchase our salvation. And He gives us the option of handing over the "pen" so that He can become the Author of our story. Allow Him to take your *mess* and use it for His *message*. He desires to become your everything.

When I think about all the stories that have occurred over the last ten years and are still occurring even today, the only way I know how to describe what it has been like to be a part of it all is through a song by Avalon. I was the person who grew up hearing all the things about God, and I even knew the Bible stories, but it wasn't until He became my everything that I began to put the missing pieces of the puzzle together. From there I learned that, although my story mattered, it was much more than my story, it was His story being written and woven in and out of mine. He became more to me...more than a story...more than words on a page. He became everything...everything to me!

Everything to Me[1]
Written by Chad Cates and Sue C. Smith
Performed by Avalon

I grew up in Sunday school
I memorized the golden rule
And how Jesus came to set the sinner free
I know the story inside out
I can tell you all about
The path that led Him up to Calvary
But ask me why He loves me
And I don't know what to say
But I'll never be the same
Because He changed my life when He became
Everything to me, He's more than a story
More than words on a page of History
He's the air that I breathe the water I thirst for
And the ground beneath my feet
He's everything, everything to me

We're living in uncertain times
And more and more I find that I'm aware
Of just how fragile life can be
I want to tell the world I've found
A love that turned my life around
They need to know that they can taste and see
Now everyday I'm praying
Just to give my heart away
I want to live for Jesus
So that someone else might see that He is
Everything to me, He's more than a story
More than words on a page of history
He's the air that I breathe, the water I thirst for
And the ground beneath my feet
He's everything and looking back over my life at the end
I'll go to meet You, saying You've been...
You're everything to me
You're more than a story
More than words on a page of history
You're the air that I breathe the Water I thirst for
And the ground beneath my feet
You're EVERYTHING,
Lord, You're everything to ME
You're everything to me, Jesus.

"To God Be the Glory for the Things He has done."

Prayers

On the next three pages, you will find prayers that you may want to pray, or you may want to pray your own prayer. There is no right or wrong way to pray. God sees the heart, and He is patiently waiting for you to come to Him.

Salvation

If you have never had a personal relationship with Jesus, it is very simple. It is a matter of believing and confessing Him as Lord. It's like having a best friend that you talk to and spend time with. That relationship will grow as you stay in prayer and read His word. Seek out new friends; it helps to stay around other believers until you are secure in who you are. You may be thinking, "That is not for me. All the people I read about in this book must have some kind of special connection." Guess what? They are all just like you; we all struggle every day, and we all are in need of a Savior. The prayer below is a simple prayer written by Joe Hill, a faithful prayer partner of the ministries.

Dear Father, I want to come to You in Jesus' name. I wish to repent and ask You to forgive me of all my sins, from the time I was born until this moment, of anything I may have said, thought, or done that is not pleasing in Your sight. I desire to ask Jesus to come into my heart and cover all my sins by His blood and wash me white as snow. I also want Jesus to fill me with His Holy Spirit, so I can carry out the purpose God created me for, now and throughout eternity, so that You can bless me and let me be a blessing, now and forevermore. Thank You, Father.

In Jesus' name, Amen

Rededication

If you have wandered away from God, and you want to rededicate your life to Him today, renewing your commitment to Him and getting your relationship back on track with Him, you may want to pray this prayer (or one of your own) from your heart.

Father in Heaven, I ask You to forgive me of my sins and cleanse me from all unrighteousness. I repent for not making You first place in my life. I know without You being Lord of my life, there is no way I can walk in victory. Anything that has become an idol, I give You permission to remove. I pray that You will renew a right spirit within me. I ask Your Holy Spirit to come and have Your way in my life. I thank You for the blood of Jesus and what He did on the cross for me. I know there is nothing I can ever do to deserve it. Thank You for loving me and paying the price for all my sins. Help me to stay on the path You set before me each and every day. Help me to hear and understand Your voice when You are speaking to me. Forgive me for being lukewarm; I am giving You permission to light a fire within me that cannot be blown out.

In Jesus Name, Amen.

Post-Abortion Prayer

If you have had an abortion, you may have experienced or may still be experiencing feelings of guilt, depression, anxiety, unexplained anger, or rage. You may have nightmares, insomnia, self-destructive behaviors, or suicidal thoughts. If you would like to be free from these things and receive forgiveness and healing, please pray this prayer (or pray your own words).

Dear Father,

I know that You were there that day. You saw my pain and confusion, and I know You cried. I know that what I did was wrong. Please, forgive me. Even now, these words are painful, and I struggle with forgiving myself. It is hard to believe that You would forgive me. But I thank You that You gave Your life so that I could live and be forgiven of all my sins! I also ask that You forgive everyone involved in the death of my baby. I pray for those who discouraged me from choosing life for my baby, and I forgive them and release them from my judgment. I thank You, Lord, for Your blood, which cleanses me from all my sins. Please help me to forgive myself for ending the life of my baby. Lord, I give to You the shattered pieces of my heart and life. That part of me that has been buried and hidden away in grief, I now lay open before You today. I give You this guilt, depression, anxiety, anger, and rage. I give them all to you, and I ask you to replace them with Your peace, Your grace, and Your love. Heal every wound. I receive Your beauty in place of my ashes. I receive Your joy in place of my mourning. I put on Your garment of praise instead of the heaviness that has weighed me down for so long. I know that my child is with You. Will You please give him/her a hug from me? And please tell him/her that I love him/her, and I look forward to our reunion one day in heaven when we will all finally be home together.

In Jesus Name I pray, AMEN.

If you would like more information on healing after abortion, there are helpful resources and websites listed under *Post Abortion* on the reference page. We pray that you will find the healing and restoration that you need. Jesus does not condemn you. He loves you. He wants to heal you and take the shattered pieces of your life and mold them together into something beautiful. He wants you to be free from the guilt and shame. He loves you.

Decision Page

If you made a first time decision to truly seek the Lord with your whole heart or rededicated your life to him, this is His promise to you, "Call to me and I will answer you; I'll tell you marvelous and wondrous things that you could never figure out on your own"(Jeremiah 33:3 MSG).

The Lord has been waiting on this day for a long time and rest assured your life will never be the same. Please email our ministry at aplace@gogenesis.com if this book has impacted your life in any way. If you now have a better understanding of how much Jesus loves you and that He wants to be your everything, we would love to hear from you. With your signature here, this will become the most important page in this book for you. Please keep this page as a reminder of your commitment to your Lord and Savior Jesus Christ. Signature _____ Date _____

For special prayer requests or to contact our ministry, visit www.aplaceforus.com or call 864-229-4243

Endnotes

Chapter 3: Turn the Radio On

1. Scott, Jimmy, and Wayne Tester. "A Place for Us." *The Fire Again*. Kim Hill. Sparrow Records, 1997. CD.
2. Meyer, Joyce. "Beauty for Ashes." *Life in the Word Devotional*. Fenton, Missouri: FaithWords, 1998. 12-13. Print. Used by Permission.

Chapter 11: Sowing Seeds of Hope

1. www.designsbyLeehee.com

Chapter 15: Leave the Miracles to Me; You Be and I'll Do

1. Roberts, Frances J. *Come Away My Beloved*. Uhrichsville, Ohio, Barbour Publishing, Inc, 1973. 159. Print. Used by Permission.

Chapter 16: All for Love

1. *Daily Walk Bible* Tyndale House Publishers, Inc.; Revised edition, 2007.

Chapter 18: Arms Wide Open

1. *The Passion of the Christ*. Dir. Mel Gibson. Perf. Jim Caviezel, Monica Bellucci and Maia Morgenstern. 20th Century Fox, 2004. DVD.

Chapter 19: Being Found

1. Graham, Billy. *God's Love for You: Hope and Encouragement for Life*. Nashville, TN: Thomas Nelson, 2007. Print.

Chapter 20: No More Shackles
1. *The Nativity Story,* Dir. Catherine Hardwicke. Perf. Keisha Castle-Hughes, Shohreh Aghdashloo and Oscar Isaac. New Line Productions, 2007. DVD

Chapter 24: Butterflies Tomorrow
1. Taken from: *The Power of a Praying ® Wife.* Copyright© 1997 by Stormie Omartian Eugene, Oregon 97402. www.harvest-housepublishers.com. Used by Permission, 106.

Conclusion: More Than a Story
1. Avalon. "Everything to Me." *Testify to Love: The Very Best of Avalon.* Sparrow Records, 2003. CD. (License #480333)

Resources

Addiction

- *The Bondage Breaker*, Neil T. Anderson, (Harvest House Publishers, 2006).
- *Victory Over Darkness*, Neil T. Anderson, (Regal, 2000).
- *The Steps to Freedom in Christ*, Neil T. Anderson, (Gospel Light, 2004).
- *Winning Spiritual Warfare*, Neil T. Anderson, (Harvest House Publishers, 1991).
- *Who I Am in Christ,* Neil T. Anderson, (Regal, 2001).
- *The Twelve Steps: A Spiritual Journey by Friends of Recovery,* Neil T. Anderson, Mike and Julia Quarles.
- *The Twelve Steps for Christians*, Friends of Recovery, (RPI Publishing; 1994).
- *When Someone You Love Abuses Drugs and Alcohol*, Cecil Murphy, (Beacon Hill Press, 2004).
- *The Life Recovery Bible NLT*, Stephen Arterburn and David Stoop, (Tyndale House Publishers; 2006).
- *Addictions- A Banquet in the Grave*, Edward T. Welch, (P & R Publishing, 2001).
- *Trapped: Mercy for Addictions*, Nancy Alcorn, (WinePress Publishing, 2008).

Adoption

- *Pregnant? Adoption is an Option*, Jeanne Warren Lindsey, (Morning Glory Press, 1997).
- *Dear Birthmother...Thank you for Our Baby*, Kathleen Silber and Phylis Speedlin, (Corona Publishing Company, 1982,1991,1997).

Eating Disorders

❖ *Starved: Mercy for Eating Disorders*, Nancy Alcorn, (Wine-Press Publishing, 2007).

Self-Harm

❖ *Cut: Mercy for Self-Harm,* Nancy Alcorn, (WinePress Publishing, 2007).

❖ *Beyond Cut: Real Stories, Real Freedom*, Nancy Alcorn, (WinePress Publishing, 2009).

Sexual Abuse

❖ *Violated: Mercy for Sexual Abuse*, Nancy Alcorn, (Wine-Press Publishing, 2008).

❖ *Rid of My Disgrace: Hope and Healing for Victims of Sexual Abuse*, Justin Holcomb and Lindsey Holcomb, (Crossway Books, 2011).

❖ *Redemption: Freed by Jesus from the Idols We Worship and Wounds We Carry*, Mike Wilkerson, (Crossway Books, 2011).

Post-Abortion

❖ *Forgiven and Set Free: A Post-Abortion Bible Study for Women,* Linda Cochrane, (Baker Books, 1996).

❖ *I Will Hold You in Heaven*, Jack Hayford, (Regal, 2003).

❖ www.postabortionsyndrome.org

❖ www.ramahinternational.org

❖ www.abortionrecovery.org

Grief

❖ *Grace for the Widow,* Joyce Rogers, (B&H Books, 2009).

❖ *Traveling Light,* Max Lucado, (Thomas Nelson 2006).

Life Changing Resources

❖ *Lies Young Women Believe*, Nancy Leigh DeMoss and Dannah Gresh, (Moody Publishers 2008).

❖ *Safe People and Boundaries*, Dr. Henry Cloud and Dr. John Townsend, (Zondervan, May 19, 2009).

- ❖ ***Boundaries***, Dr. Henry Cloud and Dr. John Townsend, (Zondervan, April 1, 1992).
- ❖ ***Boundaries With Teens,*** John Townsend, (Zondervan, 2006)
- ❖ ***Power of a Praying Wife***, Stormie Omartian, (Harvest House Publishers, 2007).
- ❖ ***Battlefield of the Mind***, Joyce Meyer, (FaithWords, 1995).
- ❖ ***God's Love for You: Hope and Encouragement for Life***, Billy Graham, (Thomas Nelson, 2007).
- ❖ ***The Purpose Driven Life***, Rick Warren, (Zondervan, 2002).
- ❖ ***The Prayer of Jabez,*** Bruce Wilkinson, (Multnomah Pub 2000).